Will You Manage?

4/95

Other ICSA Local Government titles

Local Government Financial Management
Bernard M. Jones

Local Government: The management agenda
George W. Jones

Managing Local Government Services
Derrik Hender

Will You Manage?
The Needs of Local Authority Chief Executives

Roger Morris
and
Roger Paine

ICSA Publishing
The Official Publishing Company of
The Institute of Chartered Secretaries and Administrators

First published 1995 by
ICSA Publishing Limited
Campus 400, Maylands Avenue
Hemel Hempstead
Hertfordshire, HP2 7EZ

Typeset in 10/12pt Sabon
by Hands Fotoset, Leicester

Printed and bound in Great Britain by
T.J. Press (Padstow) Ltd

British Library Cataloguing in Publication Data

A catalogue record for this book is available from
the British Library

ISBN 1-8728-6083-4

1 2 3 4 5   99 98 97 96 95

This book is dedicated to our colleagues,
whose experience and support we have
needed, relied upon and enjoyed

Contents

Foreword   xi

Preface   xiii

1 The way to the top   1

   What is a chief executive?   1
   Why be a chief executive?   3
   What does a chief executive actually do?   5
   The value of competencies   6
   Experience and self-assessment   9
   Gaining and broadening experience   10
   Continuous professional development   12
   What is SOLACE?   12

2 Just appointed   14

   The appointment itself   14
   An internal appointment   17
   An external local government appointment   19
   An external non-local government appointment   31
   The early days   31

3 The buck stops here   35

   Isolation   35
   Loneliness   37
   Being in the public eye   40
   Stress   43
   Stress and pressure   44
   The chief executive causing stress   45
   Do I relate to all this?   47

4   It's relationships that matter   **48**

The range of relationships   49
The political leaderships   50
The chief officers   57
Employees generally   61
The trade unions, the press and other key relationships   62

5   Some processes that count   **65**

Mapping the ground   65
The budget process   66
Handling negotiations   66
Employee development   67
'Managing the members'   68

6   Some ways of helping   **76**

Feedback   76
Mentoring   81
Action learning   81
Networking   83
Time management   84

7   Some frequent dilemmas   **86**

Manoeuvring   87
The chief officer who wants my job, or is too close
   to a politician   87
Civic and religious attendances   89
Who fixes the agenda?   90
How close do I get to my leader?   91
How do I allocate goodies?   92
Handling customer complaints without undermining procedures   93
The chief officer with a vested interest in privatisation   94
Should I go to party group meetings?   95
My personal publicity profile   98
Should I be the monitoring officer?   99
Should I advise on standing orders and go to council meetings?   100
My predecessor is still around   101
Should I publish management team minutes?   102
Should I live in the area?   102

8   What else has been written?   **104**

Books   104
Other materials   105

Appendix 1   Defining competencies   108

Appendix 2   SOLACE guidelines on gifts and hospitality   113

Appendix 3   Northampton guidelines for member–employee
                        relations   116

Appendix 4   One day in the life of a chief executive   119

Index   121

Foreword

'The buck stops here' is the critical learning moment for new chief executives. This timely book from Roger Morris and Roger Paine delves into what it feels like to be a chief executive. It is enriched by their personal experiences and that of many colleagues.

The role of the modern chief executive in local government is at the boundaries of unprecedented change, pressures and challenge. Old certainties cannot be relied on. This work provides a personal and practical framework for many of the dilemmas and experiences faced by chief executives. Equally important, it details methods for chief executives to find support and guidance and maintain their self-development, whether experienced or new to the challenge.

The provision of information on the legislative framework, a review of relevant publications and a careful selection of current critical issues add to the body of knowledge and understanding of the changing role of the chief executive.

This is a new and invaluable contribution to the publications that assist chief executives in their role and also help others appreciate the complexities of the task.

Judith Hunt
Chief Executive
Local Government Management Board

Preface

'Every authority is different.'

'All chief executives have similar problems.'

These are two everyday comments you hear made about the local government world of the mid-1990s. Are they really true, or just plausible generalisations? Can chief executives – or any other comparable group for that matter – usefully share recognised experiences and draw worthwhile parallels about the jobs they do, or is that simply impossible in the context of the diversity of local government and local communities which is so often proclaimed as its strength? In short, is it inconsistent to talk at the same time both about chief executive similarity and about local authority diversity, or can they indeed co-exist?

We believe they can, and do. Local government's diversity is endless, and you generalise about it at your peril. But that does not mean there aren't many facts and facets about it which are worth extracting, analysing and comparing.

So it is with chief executive jobs. They come in great variety, some 500 of them in the UK at any one time. They also come with a standard (and remarkably slender) personal legislative framework and a lot of attributes, opportunities and burdens which chief executives mutually recognise and understand. Both of us are aware of this from our involvement with groups of newly appointed chief executives organised by the Society of Local Authority Chief Executives (SOLACE).

Most new appointees seem to find that meeting others in similar positions and comparing notes with them is time well spent. Something may often be learned from differences as well as from similarities, quite apart from the permutations of empathy and sympathy that private conversation with professional colleagues seems to generate.

Being a chief executive can be described by more adjectives that you can fit on a flip chart, but one adjective in every group's list seems to be 'lonely'. This book is an attempt to recognise and restrict that loneliness, using our own experiences and sharing those of others in order to portray some of the issues and implications of life as head of the paid service.

This is not a manual. We have tried to limit the amount of advice we offer, though we hope readers will take strength from the realisation that they are not quite as alone as they thought they were. In any case, you may need the confidence, even the courage, to be different. Those who truly know the job will always respect you for that.

The fact that ultimately you and your job are unique is an argument for, and not against, making as much as you can of all the common ground you can find with your colleague chief executives. Consider yourself fortunate to hold a position of such indefinable variety, fascination and frustration that 50 or 60 hours a week will never be enough . . .

Roger Morris
Roger Paine
January 1995

Chapter 1

The way to the top

- What is a chief executive?
- Why be a chief executive?
- What does a chief executive actually do?
- The value of competencies
- Experience and self-assessment
- Gaining and broadening experience
- Continuous professional development
- What is SOLACE?

What is a chief executive?

It is now some thirty years since the title 'chief executive' first began to be used in British local government. The term, apparently American in overtones at first, is now established in all fields. Indeed, it may have become devalued by presumptuous use in small organisations. No matter – the successful local government chief executive is unlikely to be overconscious of his or her status. As a neutral, non-company way of describing the most senior employee or manager, 'chief executive' is a handy, compact phrase which has largely overcome the tautologous alternative of 'chief executive officer'.

Under the stimulus of the Bains (England and Wales) and Paterson (Scotland) Reports (see pages 14–15), the concept of a chief executive was almost universally adopted by the new authorities of 1974–75. Those authorities, indeed, adopted largely *en bloc* most of the recommendations of the two committees to a degree difficult to recognise today, when most councils are far *more* likely to find local solutions to management issues, and, of course, far *less* likely willingly to accept central government prescription not backed by statutory obligation.

As we set out more fully at the beginning of Chapter 2, from its formation in 1973 the Society of Local Authority Chief Executives (SOLACE: see pages 12–13) established as the twin qualifying attributes of a person entitled to membership that he or she, whether or not actually styled chief executive, must be both head of the paid service and principal policy adviser of the authority.

Statute during that period, however, has never formally required councils to have a chief executive as such. In recent years there have been some specific provisions of this kind (for example, section 59(1) of the Building Societies Act 1986 requiring them to have a 'chief executive', and para 11(1) of schedule 7 to the Housing Act 1988 requiring housing action trusts to have a 'chief officer'), but in local government it was 1989 before the Local Government and Housing Act that year required the appointment of a *head of the paid service* (section 4).

Throughout this book we use 'chief executive' to mean someone who is of course statutory head of the paid service, indisputably the most senior employee or manager of a given authority, and also capable of qualifying for SOLACE membership.

There is no single way, or even a few ways, of either qualifying to become, or actually becoming, a chief executive. Apart from, we suppose, a handful of direct internal promotions, the only common characteristic of all chief executives in terms of how they got the job is that they successfully answered an advertisement.

But if this flexibility sounds a good thing for local government, enabling each council freely to seek the best candidate available for the job they want to offer at the salary they are prepared to pay, it isn't much help to the aspiring candidate wanting positive advice, or to the careers adviser trying to help a potential entrant to the service who is ambitious to get to the top.

Law and practice vary quite widely across the world, in countries whose local government system is recognisably like that in Britain, as to whether chief executives need any kind of formal qualifications. There are no requirements in Britain or New Zealand, but there are in Australia, while in South Africa the office of town clerk has been particularly closely restricted by statute.

It is the clear opinion of SOLACE that the lack of any recognised or required single qualification to become a chief executive is a great strength both to the eclectic membership of the profession and to local government as a whole. This is the one top job in local government with the greatest variety of postholders and choices of route in getting there. It is also a job of infinite variety in terms of duties and activities, and a job which, as we hope this book will portray, can never be neatly compartmentalised or pinned down: a job where the skills you need are whatever go to the heart of whatever it is you ought to be doing at any time. Not for nothing do chief executives joke about 'chief executive skills' as a coded way of referring to the teasing, testing, endlessly stimulating and occasionally almost ludicrous list of things they are called upon to do to deliver the job satisfactorily.

This sort of 'job-is-what-you-make-it' flexibility is not just a recognition of the huge variety in local government between one authority and another. It is also a recognition that a wide variety of skills and approaches can validly and advantageously be applied to those authorities by chief executives of differing outlooks, character, experiences and approaches. That is why a central message of this book is about having the confidence to be your own person, to decide your own approach and be true to your own style, and not expecting to find single best practice answers to most of the professional issues and dilemmas you face. Like your staff, colleagues in other authorities can give good advice, but they do not have to carry it through as you must do. If you want to be a chief executive you must feel empowered, stimulated and confident about this kind of personal risk and exposure, and not inhibited or threatened by it.

Of course, the fact that there is no *single* recognised qualification for becoming a chief executive is not the same state of affairs as the job not needing *any* qualifications. Many chosen candidates for chief executives continue to have professional qualifications in fields which could be called 'traditional' in local government. But whether or not this is the case, clearly no one is ready to be short-listed for such a post if they cannot demonstrate a record of senior management or equivalent experience (with or without lots of letters after the name) and, moreover, experience of a breadth adequate for the range of responsibilities and skills the job requires. Local government managers are overall a highly and professionally qualified group of people. The specifications for local government's top jobs now, however, for the most part share the characteristics you would expect to find of any senior management jobs which do not by their very nature require a particular qualification.

Why be a chief executive?

For many within local government already, the inspiration or example from which they drew their ambition to be a chief executive is inevitably likely to be their own image or experience of the post as held by somebody else, what it entails and what it can offer. The role model may be a good example to which you aspire, or a less satisfactory one which brings about the self-confidence that you can do better. Either way, it serves its purpose as a catalyst to the achievement of your own goals and ambitions.

For others – and clearly this applies particularly to those not yet in local government – other materials like books, videos, visits and other experiences may provide inspiration and encouragement. Few useful generalisations are likely about these, but for this and other purposes it may be helpful to refer to some of the publications listed in Chapter 8 of this book. A particularly useful study is Chapter 7 of Janice Morphet's book *The Role of Chief Executives in Local Government* (Longman, 1993).

Why would anyone want to be a chief executive? It's a somewhat lonely, rather publicly exposed position with long hours and a wide range of tasks you can never say you've finished. We suspect that most people will quote from the following reasons (which we offer in no particular order):

- The fact that it *is* the kind of job we've just described appeals as being worthwhile.
- Power.

- Influence.
- Pay and conditions.
- A perception of job security.
- Added value.
- Commitment to public service.
- It's expected of them.
- A sense of destiny.
- A perception of social prestige.
- The appeal of a challenge.
- A logical progression from a past job or career.
- Located where one wishes to move/stay.

All too obviously some of these reasons will be more private, or will go down better at the interview, than others. For many, a combination of reasons will seem the only answer: pay, location and plausible career move will have to be considered adequate for practical reasons, but the real appetite for tackling the job will have to be based on other personal values. We would venture to say that nobody for whom such values did not form 90 per cent of the reasons for the involuntary sense of excitement on first reading the advertisement is going to find it easy to be a successful chief executive in current local government conditions. Job satisfaction is not the same as being well paid or 'being in a nice place to live'.

Whatever the combination of reasons why any particular individual seeking to become a chief executive, in our experience there are three critical qualities which any successful chief executive will be found to possess. These are:

1. A sense of perspective, proportion and judgement.
2. A sense of humour.
3. Sensational stamina, to be able to deal with the pressures and stresses.

Without the first, the discernment and experience you need to think strategically, to review and assess the advice you receive, and to continue delivering the essentials amidst a welter of details and distractions, is likely to be missing. The second is an obvious safety valve to defuse tension, especially if you can laugh at the absurdity of the things you sometimes find yourself doing, and show a human face to those around you who may otherwise be affected by your own apparently intense or worried mood. Variations from one extreme to another is a characteristic of British public life (which may help keep feet on the ground): the late Foreign Secretary, Anthony Crosland, MP for Grimsby, told Roger Morris how early one Saturday morning he met the US Secretary of State for talks at a Lincolnshire air base. After this meeting the Secretary of State took off for Washington in a special aircraft, presumably to brief the President, whereas Anthony Crosland drove himself to Grimsby to meet a constituent about his pigeon loft!

We comment later in this book (see page 44) about the value of mental safety valves in relation to stress. It's a good idea to think consciously from the outset about the problems and dangers you have observed in others, and what you can do to avoid them in yourself. Some find a particular hobby or interest a helpful outlet and release to counterbalance the restraint and degree of decorum or dignity expected of you as a chief executive. It's permissible even to have a known bias or 'thing' in a field unrelated to official duties which can serve as a small-talk icebreaker with others and an outlet or mental safety valve for you. Naturally it has to be something which will not cause offence or compromise you in any way, but deciding that is where your sense of judgement comes in.

> C.Ex was a musician who played the organ in church and took regular opportunities to pursue his hobby and particular ability. The authority's elected members never gave this a second thought. But another C.Ex at a different authority was similarly a keen and able musician, except that he was a drummer in a local band. When he was asked to resign for lack of effectiveness, it was considered that his overall image had materially contributed to the leading elected members' opinion of him.

The moral from these sorts of examples is not that the church organ is in and the drums out but that, like it or not, you will have to think about the way those whom you seek to persuade of your effectiveness perceive you (and maybe your partner), and that their perceptions will be nonetheless real for being sometimes inconsistent, unreasonable and arbitrary. Paragraph 31 of the JNC Conditions of Service for Chief Executives reads in conclusion that: 'He shall not subordinate his duty as chief executive to his private interests or put himself in a position where his duty and private interest conflict.' Yours is not the final interpretation of what this paragraph means.

Finally, sensational stamina undoubtedly is essential. For a job where the demands are unpredictable and never-ending, the hours long, many of the meetings and functions inclined to be tedious, and expectations high of your capacity for work and ability to show your face and 'be there', you will need all the mental and physical energy you can muster. Again, the right kind of applicants won't be put off by this, but the demands still have to be met and their requirements have to be sensibly reckoned with.

What does a chief executive actually do?

In the past few years a number of worthy attempts have been made to answer the questions about what a chief executive actually does, and what skills and experiences are required. Rather more ink has been spilt on describing what chief executives *ought* to be doing, and for most postholders their working hours will inevitably be a compromise between externally driven events, their own priorities and programmes, and a degree of pragmatism mixed into their responses to the often influential advice available from sources like the Local

Government Management Board, the Audit Commission, SOLACE, INLOGOV at Birmingham University and others.

In Chapter 8 of this book we list a number of recent worthwhile sources as already indicated on page 3.

What makes an effective chief executive? There may well be no single or lasting answer to such a question. By way of a starting point, however, here are the necessary attributes postulated in discussion in November 1993 by a group of chief executives, each with two or three years' experience of the job. They suggested that defining chief executive effectiveness involved the following:

1. Being able to lead on and facilitate a vision, and deal with 'the big issues'.
2. Being well respected by members and by employees generally around the authority.
3. Being well respected by one's customers and/or public, and by the wider community.
4. Having dependence on people's perception of the authority as successful in terms of image, customer satisfaction, financial prudence, and the extent of local democracy.
5. Possessing the generally recognised management competencies, as well as judgement.
6. Possessing the requisite local knowledge.

This definition is neither final nor formal in any way, but we think it provides both a starting point and a ready benchmark against which any chief executive could reasonably measure him or herself. You have to be able to make things work, and to make things happen.

We return to the theme of what chief executives actually *do* in Chapter 5.

The value of competencies

We referred in the previous section to the discussion group's point (5) about 'possessing the generally recognised management competencies'. But what exactly *are* they?

As more interest has been taken and more work been done, so increasingly results have appeared on the attributes of chief executive work and the abilities or characteristics required, or desirable, to do the job effectively. As a starting point, Appendix C of the April 1993 LGMB paper *Managing Tomorrow: Panel of inquiry report* sets out (p. 22) a list of general statements 'to describe the likely competencies needed by future managers' generally. The statements say that:

- They attempt to define the characteristics held by individuals which are brought to the occupational role.
- They are not specific to a level of management or type of job. Different jobs will require more of some competencies and less of others.

- They have not been derived by any rigorous method of analysis and will need to be tested and developed in local situations.
- They are managerial competencies, and sit beside any professional competencies required in any particular job.
- They can be used as an adjunct to those competencies developed by the management charter initiative, which focus on four key roles: managing information, managing finance, managing people, and managing operations.

The competencies themselves, each of which is defined in the following pages, are then set out as these:

- Well-developed political skills.
- Strategic management skills.
- Decision-making skills.
- Well-developed negotiation skills.
- Intellect.
- Personal integrity and flexibility.
- Well-developed people management/relationship skills.
- Well-developed communication skills.
- Well-developed influencing skills.
- Results-oriented/drive for achievement.
- Operational management skills.
- Change management skills.
- Self- and stress-management skills.
- Well-developed analysis and problem-solving skills.
- Business and commercial skills.
- Leadership skills.
- Public service orientation.

In one sense the idea of competencies is not new. It was a classic approach of old-style training programmes to require candidates gradually to acquire passes in a range of subjects (we would probably call them modules today) before receiving – perhaps after a period of practical experience – their fully certificated professional status. That has indeed continued to be the basis of acceptance into the town clerkship qualification in South Africa.

The difference is that competencies are now based much more on personal qualities and capabilities (skills) than on formally measured academically based subjects (knowledge). Accordingly they are less susceptible to teaching and learning than academic or knowledge-based attributes, and more difficult to acquire – inevitably – in advance of actually doing the job.

For this reason SOLACE attaches particular importance to the need for continuing professional development: helping chief executives to use and build on their developing experience and the past experience of others, to identify and bring out the key factors that contribute to their effectiveness, can in turn help in the preparation of others to become effective chief executives in the future.

You may find the February 1994 Local Government Management Board publication *Continuing Professional Development: Partnership for change* helpful here. Appendix 1 is extracted from a competency profile derived from work done in 1993 for the SOLACE Human Resources Panel by the Local Government Management Board.

Explanation of the term 'competency' (seemingly generally regarded as interchangeable with the commonly used 'competence') is generally dated back to 1982 and Richard Boyatzis' book *The Competent Manager: A model for effective performance* (Wiley). Boyatzis defined a competency as 'an underlying characteristic of a person . . . a motive, trait, skill, aspect of one's self-image or social role, or a body of knowledge which he or she uses'. A useful recent synopsis of the term and what it signifies was published in the article 'Competent by any other name' by Charles Woodroffe in the journal *Personnel Management* (September 1991, pp. 30–3).

In local government in the USA, led by the International City-County Management Association (ICMA), significant parallel developments have recently progressed. Aided by its Task Force on Continuing Education and Professional Development, ICMA undertook in late 1992 a *Dialogue on the Profession*, of which the first major step was a membership survey. The 'ultimate goal' of the Dialogue was to reach a consensus on 'what we need to know and how we can learn it'. The results of that survey produced a broad measure of agreement that all of 27 identified 'practices' were essential – the membership reportedly opposed use of the term 'competency', so that an alternative had to be found.

This is not the place to follow the ICMA work in detail but in late 1993 a further membership survey was carried out on the next steps. Guidance was sought on what was seen by the task force as a dilemma for the profession, granted that the 1992 survey had identified the 27 practices, had broadly agreed on methods of delivery to be used 'to assist ourselves in individual professional development', and had also agreed that there would be no certification of individual members by ICMA: 'The focus is on ongoing professional development, not meeting one-time or minimum qualifications.'

The dilemma was summarised as follows in the Preface to the 1993 membership survey:

Our concern is that we've left ourselves on the horns of a professional dilemma:
- If we agree on the skills and abilities we must have in our professional role in order to make democracy work;
- If we agree on a delivery system;
- If we agree to focus on our own individual development plans, thereby demonstrating that we are a learning profession;
- If we do all this and are not willing to tell anybody;
- Then we have put ourselves in jeopardy as a profession.

Appendix 1 further lists the 27 practices identified from the 1992 membership survey and printed as Figure A in the 1993 survey. To this we have attached the Dialogue issues summary set out on page 7 of the November–December 1993 International Edition of the ICMA *Newsletter* (ICMA has members worldwide, including some in the UK, where the subordinate European CMA is based).

Experience and self-assessment

Until, perhaps, the beginning of the 1980s there was a contrast between typical attitudes to experience and to professional or technical qualifications.

It was generally accepted that experience by its very nature grew with the passage of time, and that it could often be regarded or evaluated as equalling or surpassing what are often disparagingly referred to as 'paper qualifications'. When new professional qualifications were established and the examining or regulatory mechanisms set up, existing practitioners of certain years' standing were generally admitted into the ranks.

Qualifications, on the other hand, tended to be regarded as akin to swimming or riding a bicycle: once acquired, they were capable of being held for life without automatic re-assessment or renewal, no matter how many years had passed. While the knowledge might change or evolve, the core of the professional skills or status did not. Only in recent years, and comparatively slowly, has it become generally accepted that few if any jobs will in future remain the same for a lifetime, and that continuous, or at least continual, professional development is necessary in the interests both of the practitioners and their clients or customers and also of the regulatory body whose quality standards and assessments they must meet.

In local government, SOLACE recognises the value of experience but at the same time underlines the importance of continuing personal development work to help an individual keep up with, and adapt to, changing circumstances. This also helps to keep a freshness of approach which so easily becomes stale in the endless round of meetings, commitments and long hours at the municipal grindstone.

In an ideal world there would be a set of development modules which would acquaint individuals with both (1) a means of assessing themselves and how they were doing, and (2) a means of developing their skills.

Increasingly, as the need for these requirements is recognised in today's ever more rapidly changing work environment, more opportunities are becoming available. In Chapter 6 we discuss some particular kinds of things which may be helpful.

Nevertheless, the mainspring for your own involvement in this must be your own efforts. Unless you recognise the need to build in appropriate space and time for personal development, for example, other pressures and commitments will sweep it aside. This is not something that the elected members or your subordinates are likely to force upon you, or arrange entirely suitably for you. Nor is it something that is in any way an optional extra or an admission of failure, any more than stripping down an engine from time to time would necessarily imply failure of design or a failing of performance. It is not always understood that this is so.

> C.Ex, not long after his appointment at the age of 35, asked leading councillors' approval (as was required) for him to undertake a management development programme. It was refused, a leading councillor writing him a note to the effect that 'we appointed you because you said (and we accepted) that you were up to the job. You're not supposed to come needing any more training'.

You need to allow also for the likely possibility that you do not recognise in yourself areas where development, help, improvement or the filling of a skills gap are needed. Your own assessment of your performance and effectiveness and that of others (particularly the leader) are two different things, as was very well illustrated by the Local Government Management Board study carried out with the SOLACE Human Resources Panel (April 1992) entitled *Chief Executives' Development Effectiveness* (see section 1). We return to this theme of effectiveness and what else has been written about the job of chief executive in Chapters 5 and 8.

Gaining and broadening experience

Many people successfully achieve appointment as chief executive within the authority where they are already working. We discuss the pros and cons of internal appointments in the next chapter (pages 17–19). A much smaller number, particularly those with more than a decade or so of local government service, will never have worked for any other local authority. We think you can divide relevant experience into three fairly obvious main categories.

The first category involves working for more than one authority. This may not be an absolute prerequisite of success (for how else could people manage to be appointed directly into the role of chief executive from outside the local government service altogether and acquit themselves well?). Nevertheless, you are unlikely to appreciate the reality of local government's diversity until you have worked for more than one authority and observed the different attitudes, approaches and procedures which can govern the handling of apparently similar circumstances and issues covered by identical legal requirements. Local authorities have always extensively exchanged people between them – perhaps more so in the past than in today's economic and social circumstances – and overall all sides have been much the better for it. It goes without saying that prudent job applicants do not just apply only for vacancies in which they are seriously interested and which will positively contribute to their career plan by logically extending their experience and knowledge base; they also consider how they would be placed to apply for the next job after this one if they successfully get it. Career progression cannot only be viewed from one move behind.

The second kind of experience contrast is obtained by working not just in another authority but in another sector. A decade or less ago, we in local government heard much about the private sector and how similar to it we ought to be in terms of philosophy and outlook. Rather less is heard of that theory of sameness now, which might seem ironic in view of the emphasis on a contractual atmosphere and market-tested service delivery approach which has so characterised the way things have moved over the past decade.

In fact it is not so ironic. We would argue that a by-product of all the contract testing and tendering activity, with the revolution of attitudes and approaches which it has engendered in authorities, has been a realisation that the public and private sectors are *not* ultimately the same, and cannot be treated as if they are without inappropriate consequences which cannot be supported. In truth, they may have – or maybe ought to have – more in common than people used generally to assume, but they are not *identical*. Accordingly they cannot convincingly be made to appear so, even if the competitive, customer service-driven outlook of the private sector has significantly affected public sector attitudes for the better, and even if some of the standards of social responsibilities and wider accountability developed in the public sector could sometimes be imported with advantage into some largely mercenary private sector organisations.

The local authority chief executive with direct personal experiences across this divide, wide or narrow as you make it, will have the great advantage of first-hand opinion and the chance to be constructively influenced by factors which others can only approach less closely.

Finally, *the third category* involves obtaining experience by other means than through a full employment commitment, namely by such means as second-ments, personal acquaintance or friendship, and overseas exchanges.

The above means vary as widely as you care to define them but they offer in common the opportunity for you to refocus your normal point of view by observing closely (and at least to some degree from the inside) your role or job and how it may be carried out in a different context and with a different philosophy or set of assumptions.

Although bodies like SOLACE increasingly try to offer exchange programmes and similar opportunities, these are inevitably limited compared with the total of potential beneficiaries. Once again, we would urge that you should deliberately try to find space in your own development programme for opportunities of this kind. We think it is likely to prove worthwhile beyond your expectations, whether as part of your conscious preparations for the role of chief executive or your considered full exploitation of that role once you have obtained a chief executive post and established yourself.

Continuous professional development

In this introductory chapter, we have tried to make three principal points:

1. That there is no single recognised qualification for, or single recognised way of becoming, a chief executive, so that you are free to form your own.
2. That this freedom should be sensibly used to construct a deliberate career plan or CV of qualifications and experience which will fit you for an exceptionally wide-ranging and demanding (but also therefore rewarding) job.
3. That parallel experiences and exposures are of particular value but that you are going to have to take the initiative yourself to gain the impetus you need for success.

Both your career and your life are a progression of continuous professional and personal development. This is no mere piece of homespun philosophy to set beside John Maynard Keynes' famous remark that 'in the long run we are all dead'. It is simply a reminder that both before and during your tenure of a chief executive job you need to be thinking about the wider implications and fitting them into your overall life plan. It is sensible to think (see page 10 above) about how you might move on *out of* that next job as well as *into* it. So is thinking (however cursorily) about life after chief executiveship. This no more implies dissatisfaction with, or disloyalty to, the present than does any other form of forward planning. But remarkably few of us have even the most rudimentary life plan or carry out any form of recognisable career management. Still fewer have an exit strategy from their career as it approaches its end or reaches a major change.

A trait of the Japanese character is to recognise that they are continuously learning. The rapidly changing patterns of work and living make that a desirable trait for all of us to consider, but it is particularly important for someone who faces the changes and challenges of chief executiveship.

In the following chapters we discuss a variety of aspects of the job, how it feels to do it and how you can derive support and practical help in staying on top from colleagues and other sources. That way you can both create – and re-create – the role that you and your authority need you to fulfil at all times.

What is SOLACE?

As indicated on page 1, the Society of Local Authority Chief Executives was founded in 1973 in the run up to the reorganisation brought about by the Local Government Act 1972. To be eligible, its applicants must be both the head of the paid service and the principal policy adviser of their employing local authority.

SOLACE is unique in that its membership includes all principal UK local authorities in England, Northern Ireland, Scotland and Wales, and it is the only professional association specifically for all such chief executives. Its objects, taken from its constitution, are threefold:

1. To consider any matter affecting local government and in particular the role and responsibilities of chief executives and when appropriate to take action on such matters and to present views thereon to such bodies and persons as may be appropriate.
2. To promote the knowledge, skill and competence of members in pursuance thereof to carry out research, to run conferences or courses and publish literature and otherwise to engage in or join with others in research and educational activities.
3. To do such other matters or things and to join with such other bodies or persons as may be conducive to the attainment of the general objects of the society or to be considered by the executive Council to be in the interests of the body of members as chief executives of local authorities.

Any organisation's formal objects are apt to sound worthy but dull. SOLACE has been debating its future role, the state of its membership and its resourcing for some time. There has recently been an increasing emphasis on the potential for commercial activities like the recruitment and selection service, the interim management service and the briefing courses for new chief executives. Activities overseas have developed to the point where a separate company, SOLACE International (1992) Ltd, was formed to undertake those commitments.

SOLACE offers an informal counselling service or help line for those who want to use it. The Association of Local Authority Chief Executives, ALACE, is a registered trade union for chief executives in SOLACE membership. Its representatives comprise the staff side of the Joint Negotiating Committee (JNC) for Chief Executives. The JNC's procedures relating to redundancy, capability and discipline of chief executives were recently revised for England and Wales following the Local Authorities (Standing Orders) Regulations 1993, S.I. No. 202 (see also page 16), and were published in a JNC Circular dated 28 September 1993. In consequence paragraphs 41–52 of the conditions of service have since been revised accordingly. Paragraph 7 of the Local Government Changes for England (Staff) Regulations 1995, SI No. 520, partly modify the 1993 Regulations in relation to chief executive appointments in reorganised authorities.

The SOLACE Foundation dates in concept from 1984 and is an educational trust furthering the study and well-being of local government both in the UK and internationally.

Chapter 2

Just appointed

- The appointment itself
- An internal appointment
- An external local government appointment
- An external non-local government appointment
- The early days

The routes by which people arrive at the moment of appointment as a chief executive can be categorised into three groups. They may already work for the authority, they may work elsewhere in local government (most probably at chief executive or chief officer level in another authority), or they may come from somewhere outside local government. Each of these three has its own implications, advantages and disadvantages for the successful applicants.

The appointment itself

Before discussing the routes leading to selection, the act and mechanism of appointment itself must be considered. Being offered a chief executive's job is likely to prove a memorable moment in anyone's life. In the emotion of a career peak or highlight rounding off all that has gone before, it is easy for down-to-earth details to be underestimated or overlooked altogether. Most but not all such posts use the words 'chief executive', sometimes combined with other words implying either the civic tradition of a clerkship or town clerkship or the dual possession of a discrete extra responsibility of a departmental nature.

From its founding in 1973, for SOLACE the twin hallmarks of a chief executive post have been that the holder has been both the head of the paid service and principal policy adviser of a principal local authority as defined in section 270(1) of the Local Government Act 1972. These characteristics are spelt out in the Bains Report *The New Local Authorities: Management and structure* (HMSO, 1972), Appendix J. Appendix J is built around the first part of Chapter 5 of the Bains Report, particularly pages 40–4 on the role, background and training necessary for the post. More than 20 years later, the Bains era may seem somewhat dated, going back as it does to a time when very few chief executive posts existed. You can form your own views about whether the contemporary good sense it contains is still relevant and whether the attempt to draw on private sector management experience wasn't in some respects ahead of its time. To this day the structures of many authorities can be traced to Bains and its influence, which was very great indeed when the new authorities were first elected in 1973.

The equivalent Scottish reorganisation took effect on 16 May 1975 and Scotland had its own version of Bains: the Paterson Report, *The New Scottish Local Authorities: Organisation and management structures* (HMSO, Edinburgh, 1973). There the chief executive concept is the subject of paras. 4.29–4.35, and what are called the 'terms of reference' for the chief executive comprise Appendix 11. The terms also contain the twin elements of head of paid service and principal policy adviser (although Paterson interestingly gave two exceptions to the former attribute where 'principal officers are exercising responsibilities imposed on them by statute' and 'the professional discretion or judgement of the principal officers is involved').

Bains' Appendix J and Paterson's Appendix 11 cannot be regarded as necessarily the norm today but they remain the obvious ancestors of many a current job description. It's worth spending a few minutes reflecting on that job description because officially it maps out what your new employer expects of you. Clearly you want to know whether the job description has been revised and tailored to the vacancy you applied for or is simply a rerun of what has gone before. We return to the possible differences between what 'the council' officially tells you it wants and what those in political power actually want on pages 26–7 below.

Paperwork and documentation surrounding chief executive recruitment and appointment procedures come good, bad and indifferent. The authority may be using headhunters, consultants or assessors of some kind, or they may not. They may be following the advice of a publication like *Recruiting and Selecting a Chief Executive: Guidelines for good practice* (SOLACE/LGTB, 1989), or they may not. Obviously the person appointed must check carefully through the terms and conditions of service offered and not rush to sign in the glow of pleasure at appointment. The new chief executive's influence and leverage on those terms may never be so strong again as at that time. The chief executives' registered trade union is the Association of Local Authority Chief Executives (you have to be a member of SOLACE to join ALACE). Because fixed-term contracts present particular pitfalls from the employee's point of view, ALACE has published a booklet entitled *Fixed-term Contracts for Chief Executives* by Bill Miles and Roger Morris (July 1992).

SOLACE now emphasises strongly the crucial importance of a rigorous selection process properly based on equal opportunity principles. Such a vital appointment may be irreparably weakened if not undertaken with great care and to the highest standards based on the best obtainable candidate. In furtherance of these principles SOLACE now markets its own recruitment and selection service (in association with the Local Government Management

Board) to offer local authorities the requisite advice and assistance in recruiting a chief executive or other senior officer.

From a candidate's point of view, an interview for a chief executive post can be a daunting experience. These days, following on from the previous paragraph about a rigorous selection process, you should expect rather more than just a formal interview (though for some authorities that still, more or less, apparently suffices). Psychometric testing and the use of a broad spectrum of approaches through what are called *assessment centres* are increasingly common (you may find it helpful to read the Local Government Management Board's publication *Best Practice in Management and Selection: A guide to the use of assessment centres in local government* (1992) for a clearer idea of what they involve).

Apart from all the information you can glean – referred to in the following pages – do not neglect the value of contacts and other people who may tell you more about the area and the perception of the authority itself. (But if you aren't already familiar with local government, take note of the general rule, included in many advertisements and standing orders, that canvassing disqualifies, and don't overstep the bounds of what is acceptable.)

Section 4 of the Local Government and Housing Act 1989 requires that all authorities have a statutory head of the paid service. The powers and duties attaching to that role *per se* are rather narrowly drawn and unlikely to correspond with your concept of your chief executive role. The powers of section 4(3) (about co-ordination of functions and staffing requirements), for example, may nevertheless be influential for your position even if very sparingly used. The head of the paid service will automatically be politically restricted under section 2 of that Act and may also be either the monitoring officer or chief financial officer, but not both. A number of commentaries on these nuts-and-bolts provisions exists (e.g. *Local Government Ground Rules* by R. J. B. Morris, Longmans, 1990) and it may be useful to have ready access to one of these. A measure of protection from arbitrary disciplinary action is provided by the Local Authorities (Standing Orders) Regulations 1993, S.I. No. 202 (see also page 13).

Chief executives' pay and conditions of service are regulated by a separate Joint Negotiating Committee for Chief Executives. The terms and conditions are published in booklet form, supported by joint circulars from time to time. It's also very likely that there is a considerable list of powers and delegations, 'proper officer' functions and the like, attaching to the chief executive post. The formal powers must be open to inspection under section 100G(2) of the Local Government Act 1972. The scope of this list may tell you quite a lot about the way the authority has actually been administered hitherto.

Even more revealing will be the other powers (and limitations) of the post. Look at and list them for yourself if you possibly can. While only practical experience will teach you the unwritten boundaries of member expectations, or your political authority or backing, you need to know how 'the system', instinctively maintaining its continuity in the flow of paper to your office, is likely to assume you will be working.

> C.Ex found the members expected him to present each month a list of all documents to which the common seal had been attached, a hangover from clerkship days. Choosing the moment in committee presented by an unusually long list, he obtained agreement to stop a pointless exercise with which he had no day-to-day involvement anyway. It never returned.
>
> Other C.Exs found they were supposed to counter-sign authority every time any employee went outside the authority boundary on official duties, and every time any employee undertook any formal training commitment. These essentially departmental or time-management matters added nothing of value to the C.Ex's personal control or knowledge, and were both tactfully abolished during the 'honeymoon' period.

Chief executives commonly say that they have never referred to their service conditions or job descriptions during their years in the job. Indeed, it is quite likely that you will only want to do so if something goes wrong or you want to leave. However, a small investment of time at the outset – before you get sucked into the job itself and the endless reading involved – will ensure that if you ever do reach for the small print you will find it says what you always thought it did.

An internal appointment

Much work has been done in recent years to analyse the personal and developmental characteristics of chief executives (pages 6–9 in Chapter 1, Chapter 8 and Appendix 1 refer to some of the sources). Whether an appointment is internal or external to the authority seems to get less attention than factors such as age, sex or professional background. The significance of this factor is underrated. The experience of SOLACE's work in helping new chief executives is that being an internal appointee makes a crucial difference to the waiting and starting periods. It presents its own dilemmas, as well as some obvious advantages, and clearly it is likely to be the dilemmas or drawbacks which will require thoughtful handling.

Let's start with the advantages, which will probably include some at least of the following:

- Existing knowledge of the authority and community.
- Existing knowledge by the authority of whom they have chosen.
- No family or housing disturbance required, removing relocation costs for both sides and reducing domestic matters which can preoccupy the new appointee.
- Speedier take-up where necessary, because notice periods can be disregarded.

- Perhaps demonstrates career progression or willingness to promote within the authority.

They sound like a smooth and trouble-free passage into the top job without the external, but far from peripheral, problems of housemoving, a partner's career or the children's education: the sorts of issues which – as younger appointees commonly have working partners and school-age children – distract them from concentrating all their energies on the new job, and may well give rise to tensions or feelings of guilt about the apparent selfishness of uprooting the rest of the family.

For some, the assumption of the chief executiveship may indeed be smooth. Certainly you need to be able to concentrate all your mental and physical energies for a short period on getting to grips with it. Some chief executives, however, have identified considerable problems of adjustment which they experienced in moving over internally into their new roles. These have included:

1. Finding that the job was in fact significantly different from what it had previously been perceived to be, even by experienced chief officers close to the previous postholder.
2. Finding that members consciously wanted the successor to behave very similarly to, or very differently from, the predecessor but had never made this clear.
3. Finding the loneliness or divorce from a previously comfortable professional base unnerving.
4. Finding it difficult to change relationships with formerly equal colleagues, particularly if they were disappointed candidates themselves.
5. Finding it difficult after long service in one authority to be accepted by members and officers who remember you as much younger and more junior, and who consequently find it hard to accept your accumulated experience or maturity for what it now is.
6. Finding difficulty in changing direction or being 'your own person' after years of loyal commitment to the status quo as part of the corporate management process led by a predecessor.
7. Finding that an initially attractive merger of chief executive departmental functions with those of a previous chief officer post is not sustainable because of the workload or conflicting loyalties.
8. Finding, perhaps, that having been an acting chief executive for any length of time has removed the possibility of a 'honeymoon period' and the special opportunities to signal changes that go with it.
9. Experiencing unease (in yourself or your partner) at the civic profile of the job or the time it takes.

The nine kinds of reality instanced above are, by their nature, likely to take time to show. Any that you do experience may in fact not be visible or identifiable to those around you in the authority. There are issues here that form part of what we say at pages 35–7 and 43–4 below about the intrinsic isolation and pressures of the job. Perhaps what we say about the experiences of the early days of actually doing the job (pages 31–4) will be helpful.

It's important to realise that having difficulties (and even struggling with some of them) is not unique or even unusual. It's well within the range of normal expectations and experiences of new chief executives in all kinds of authorities. Indeed, some degree of fear in the early days is natural: the converse of that would be cockiness.

The one thing that seems bound to change immediately for the internally appointed chief executive is attitude. The standpoint from which you consider the authority will be different, but for you that inner change is both recognised and realistic. Everyone else in the authority will begin to change their attitude to you too, but such change may not be discernible to you for a considerable time. The office grapevine will long since have quoted odds and opinions on your candidature for the job, and may also have built unrealistic expectations or images around you. Past friendships may grow more distant and new confidences arise: adjustments are to be expected. Your own stance will have to be established quickly, firmly and tactfully; it would be confusing, to say the least, to be sending out signals of new head-of-the-paid-service leadership one minute and 'this won't change my way of life, I'm still the same person underneath' the next.

The change of attitude may be very quick as news of your appointment is transmitted around but that does not mean you have no time. Unless promoted unexpectedly, you will have had a week or two prior to interview to prepare for it and to think about how you will react if you are offered the job. You may be about to give a first impression – do not miss the chance to envisage what it will be.

An external local government appointment

The traditional mental picture of a chief executive appointment is probably that of an experienced chief officer of one authority, perhaps with 20 years or more of varied local government service, being appointed as chief executive of another. Obviously it isn't universal, but it still is common. The backgrounds of people appointed like this vary much more widely than once they did.

The Local Government Management Board published a *Chief Executives' Development Survey* in February 1993 which gives a good deal of interesting information. The average age at appointment was 41, the average age of all current chief executives 49, and the average length of local government service 26 years (p. 9). These two paragraphs quoted from p. 15 of the survey set the scene:

Most chief executives (69%) were in chief officer posts prior to their posts, whilst the remainder came from other chief executive posts (16%), other local government posts (12%) or from outside local government (3%).

The main career backgrounds are still either legal (40%), finance (15%) or administration and management (15%). The proportion of chief executives from other backgrounds has increased from 22% to 30% since 1987; the main ones are planning (7%) and a wide range of others including engineering, environmental health, surveying, housing, leisure and recreation.

The survey on which these conclusions are based was carried out in late 1991 by the LGMB and the SOLACE Human Resources Panel, when some 36% of all chief executives then in post responded. The whole report is of considerable interest.

If you have been externally appointed, you will probably have some three months available before your starting date. Should it be decided that you'll start sooner, well and good; a much longer period may be rather unsettling. A combination of your notice period and the circumstances of your predecessor leaving office will yield an agreed date.

The importance of this date is self-evident and you ought to plan carefully, not only for how you'll actually start (see pages 31–4 below) but for how to get the best out of your notice or waiting time. It's very likely that your new job will mean a house move and that in turn will mean a job, school or friends move for other members of your family. For different reasons all of these may prove quite difficult and distracting. Their achievement and your smooth transition into your new job are closely interlinked – something you will surely recognise as you settle down after the euphoria of being appointed to the reality of what you've actually done. Even a 'dream move' back to the area of your upbringing, for example, should be respected for the considerable undertaking it represents.

Quite probably, in mentally preparing and taking yourself through your application and interview, you will have made an informal kind of SWOT analysis – strengths, weaknesses, opportunities, threats – of yourself in relation to the post and the authority. That kind of approach or process can usefully continue as you think yourself forward into your new role.

If you already are a chief executive, the status itself will not be a novelty. You already know what sorts of things being a chief executive involves and that fact is likely to have been material in your selection. An analogy is that of an experienced driver who takes out an unfamiliar car: it looks and feels different but it works overall in the same way, and general road sense does not have to be relearned. A recent survey suggested that as many as 17 per cent of newly appointed chief executives were in fact existing chief executives from other authorities.

Most appointees, however, will not have been chief executives already. If you are in this position, the waiting period before you actually start the job is particularly important. Suggesting a list of 'induction' activities is necessarily risky because any menu of competencies must take account of what you know already. Nevertheless, here are 13 possible areas of conscious preparation you may like to consider:

1. The economic profile of the area.
2. Any special industries/activities/problems/characteristics of the area or the authority itself on which you will have to develop expertise (and about which the local press will probably ask you straight away).
3. The management structure and budget of the authority.
4. All you can get hold of about the proper officer appointments, powers, delegations, authorities and so on that you need given to you personally to exercise.
5. How to get to know people in the area and who first.
6. The historical background of your area.
7. The extent of civic commitments and what will be expected of you.
8. Who will be your immediate personal staff and what they're putting in your diary for the first couple of months.
9. What priorities (if any) members gave you for when you start.
10. What priorities to give yourself for when you start.
11. What agendas, minutes, reports and so on to start seeing regularly.
12. How you want to shape your personal style, management approach and example in the job.
13. How you project your personal image as a new chief executive.

We can say a few words about each of these thirteen broad areas in time: you will need and want to make some priority choices within these headings themselves, which are not in any particular ranking order.

1. The economic profile of the area

The easiest way to add to the background preparation you did for your interview is probably to ask the appropriate officer or department in the new authority to let you have a short briefing paper.

Key indicators are not confined to demographic analysis, ward or electoral division unemployment rates and a list of the 10 biggest employers. It will be worthwhile to get some idea of any areas or projects with special status, special government money or partnership arrangements, and of other factors such as trends in crime statistics which may significantly affect the perceptions of people or the profitability of enterprises in the area. And these days there is often additional promotional material such as videos to see (though you must beware that they don't give only the gloss without the reality). That way you can make sure you visit early on – even if only on a drive-through basis – places in the authority you realise you'll have to get to know particularly well. Most people will probably react positively to being one of the first people being asked to brief the new chief executive but it isn't just a question of brownie points (necessary though a stock of these is): you can begin to judge how the authority does things. If your briefing is slow, poorly produced and not well focused around what you have asked or clearly should be told, it's a bad sign for everyone else who doesn't command the quality of response you expect.

At the same time you don't want to be awash with paper. You won't spot or retain the essentials anywhere near so easily and at this stage the essentials are really all you want.

2. Any special industrial activities/problems/characteristics of the area or the authority

This is clearly linked with (1), and yet goes wider. If you are going to a seaside resort, a new town, a port or whatever, you will want to think about and be briefed on issues and aspects which are unfamiliar. You could get chief or other senior officers to take you round and interpret the issues for you. Equally there may be issues of paramount local importance – say, for example, a new car plant, traditional industry closures or the impact of Channel Tunnel infrastructure – which you can see from the outset will soon require sufficient expertise on your part to enable you to advise, speak publicly, and probably give strategic leads within the authority as well. Issues like these will command your attention like overdue questions in a crowded examination syllabus: they are bound to come up very soon. But this is not just about issues: there may be organisations or activities unique or special to the area to which similar considerations apply.

3. The management structure and budget of the authority

Just as you are unlikely to feel you are even beginning to familiarise yourself until you have got to know your immediate colleagues and staff, so you are unlikely to feel fully confident about the authority's budget until you have been in post for sufficient time to go through a complete revenue estimates process.

Since reading staff and budget printouts is a tedious business without a particular purpose, create one. Compare establishment or budget figures with ones you're used to; look at the way they show overheads or recharges, or whatever: anything which will help you familiarise yourself with the style and approach. The same sort of method may be helpful as and when you can get access to computer-held budget data or other information systems. A particularly useful source is the Audit Commission authority profile work on 'family' comparators.

4. Proper officer appointments, and powers, delegations, authorities, etc. you can exercise

These may be revealing: by no means every authority has the systematic and up-to-date lists they ought to have. This kind of thing may seem like trivia and it's true that record keeping is a nuts-and-bolts kind of task. It ceases to be trivia if you get a challenge and find that the authority minutes you believed were there aren't (and if that's true for you, it's likely to be true also for other proper officers and people who exercise delegations). So while they check your references, you check their authorisations!

There's another reason for doing this. It may help you to start building up that necessary feel for what you can and can't do in the authority and help you find out how narrow or wide is the trust that authority members will be actually placing in you (and/or probably placed in your predecessor). As lists of delegations often grow, prompted by specific problems or incidents, ambivalences may occur. You might be pleased to find entrepreneurial freedom to manage the council's land assets, for example, contrasting oddly with the need to certify every occasion when some employee goes outside the authority boundary for some reason.

> Well into his second year, C.Ex was challenged by a member as to his authority to act as monitoring officer. No minute could be found for his principal C.Ex appointment (which had taken place in a recess), let alone the monitoring officer role. His appointment was valid, but had to be inferred from references in other documents and evidently he had never personally checked or regularised his position.

5. How to get to know people in the area, and who first

A very obvious starting point for introductions is your own immediate office. They will be curious, at the least, about the style and temperament of the new individual (for whom these things are likely to have more immediate relevance day-to-day than your policy choices or knowledge of managerial philosophy).

This immediate circle can be widened to include management team colleagues, political leaders and those who chair key committees, as well as any others whose positions seem specially prominent for any reason *vis-à-vis* your own. You want to be visible; you may even want to provide a 'surgery' for members generally.

Already, however, the list may be too ambitious; after you have taken up your job you will have more time to develop contacts, who may in the event be more forthcoming and revealing with you after your predecessor has actually departed. We set out on pages 32–3 below a list of some of the other agencies or people in the community with whom one group of newly appointed chief executives felt early contact was desirable. Doing much about that may well be difficult before you actually start but a lot of these external contacts can be useful (and even essential) in the early days in giving their perceptions of the local authority.

Before taking up post you may judge the priority to be consciously to try above all to make a good impression. Your ambivalent position – already privileged, yet still outside the system – may be advantageous, allowing you to pose 'silly questions' or elicit information or comments which may not be so easily done once you have become part of the establishment and people's responses are less relaxed because of the aura of chief executiveship which is likely to surround even the most approachable postholder in the eyes of subordinates.

It is particularly important, before starting the job, to have met the political leaders (and perhaps even the political groups) to get yourself better known, to demonstrate commitment and to pick up signals about what ticks. This is a time to take in all you can but at the same time to keep control, often to keep your own counsel, to be bold and to start with people as you mean to go on.

6.   The historical background of your area

Whilst some authorities are more obviously 'historical' than others, every area clearly has its traditions and associations. An outline knowledge of them, at least, should be part of your stock in trade and whatever your best endeavours it is likely to be harder, the longer time goes on, to sit down to read that worthy civic history.

The area's history and attractions are not only relatively easily and enjoyably absorbed at the outset as part of the pleasure of being given the job, they may also help you directly to understand what part they play in the policies, programmes and commitments of the authority itself.

7.   The extent of your civic commitments

Of all aspects of your new job, the civic side is one which, unless you are already involved with it, is most easily underestimated. It is also likely to involve considerable commitments and local visibility for your partner.

Although the significance and civic profile of the position will vary greatly from place to place, the time taken up by civic commitments may well be considerable and, of course, will largely be outside office hours. As the average age of chief executives has gradually reduced, so the likelihood has increased that both partners have work commitments and/or children of baby-sitting ages. Factors such as these simply add to all the usual concerns about long hours, social drinking, stress or whatever.

In some quarters it may be fashionable to decry the social and civic sides of the job (even though there are likely to be occasions which are both a pleasure and privilege to attend). If your job title retains the clerk or town clerk style as well, it is probably a good indicator that this aspect of the job remains significant in the members' eyes.

We say more about undertaking and surviving the civic side of life as head of the paid service on pages 89–90. At this pre-start stage it will be well to diary the essential or expected commitments and make some estimate of what other functions you think it useful or politic to attend. A balance has to be struck between making a particular introductory effort to put yourself around in the early days (which may seem quite attractive if perhaps you are temporarily having to live away from home prior to moving to your new locality) and not setting such a pace or precedent that you cannot keep it up and accordingly convey a fading impression.

You must make your assessment of the civic officer or secretary very soon, so that you can decide how much concern for this kind of work and organisation you can safely delegate and rely on being properly done. The word 'work' is used advisedly: civic functions are a duty for you and whatever your terms and conditions or fond images of time in lieu may be, they should be respected accordingly. A good test of whether something that comes your way is or is not 'work' is whether you would be doing it if you did not hold the position you do.

8. Your personal staff and your diary for the first couple of months

On one level this is again an obvious matter. There will seem to be little doubt about who occupies the posts of personal or executive assistant secretary and so on. There is, nevertheless, good reason to look at the relevant job descriptions and the way the people have been used to working in the past. After all they are personal staff and your predecessor's approach is unlikely closely to match your own. The skills of the person or people in post now may not be best suited to what you expect. Any doubts about this must surface as soon as possible, because personal staff are part of your eyes and ears, and inevitably the impressions you and your chief executiveship give are closely bound up with the impression they give.

> C.Ex inherited two posts known prior to his arrival as 'aides'. They were excellent staff capable of (and later receiving) more senior responsibilities, yet their 'duties' included acting as drinks waitresses at civic receptions and doing a variety of personal shopping errands for the predecessor C.Ex. Activities of this nature varied from being not cost effective to clearly inappropriate and had to be quietly discontinued. It became clear that what the predecessor had been allowed to get away with, the successor C.Ex would not have been had he tried to continue the old ways.

The point about the diary is particularly important. Those first couple of months will be your honeymoon period when considered reports or action are not really expected from you, you are not yet sucked into the endless daily round, and you need to use all the space and time you can get for your induction process and priorities. Avoid at all costs being submerged by other people's agendas or by trivia and/or firefighting. You will not want that time to be taken away from you any more than is inevitable and, as with so many other things, in the realm of time management you will probably have made new resolutions for yourself and will want to start as you intend to go on.

It is particularly important to have time allocated to meet people who have expectations (Who is he/she? What is he/she like?) about the new chief executive and to meet people from all walks of the authority's workforce.

Time management (see pages 84–5), a key issue for all top managers, is particularly important for chief executives because:

- The pressures on them are greater.
- They need to set an example for the rest of their managers.
- Time management and stress problems can be related, so that if things are not to build up unacceptably it is essential from the outset to block out periods of free time.

9.   What priorities (if any) members gave you

Some job advertisements, or the package of information that's available to enquirers about them, make clear that one or more key tasks await the successful applicant.

Often the objective quoted is as soft or meaningless as political backing for any specific action. It sounds exhilarating to lead the authority into the twenty-first century or face the challenges of growing public concern about the environment, but such idealism or platitudes do little to empower the subsequent postholder and certainly don't answer the hard-edged question 'What do they actually want me to *do*?'

Perhaps in specific terms they don't actually *know* and it's part of your role to tell them, get their approval, and then go forward in the chosen way. Alternatively it may be quite clear that if they haven't found the answer, they certainly know what they perceive their problem to be: to reform the management structure, reduce overheads, restore public confidence in some services, or whatever. This empowers your position but also equally creates a specific, as opposed to a general, expectation about your programme and performance in the early months. Your attitude to this may well vary from welcoming the focus and the given choice of priority, to feeling committed and boxed in by parameters you have neither set nor assessed yourself.

A variation on this is the situation where no discernible priorities are given to you at all, so that your reaction might be more or less the opposite of that posed at the end of the previous paragraph. You may, perhaps, be very conscious of a lack of political focus but conversely also welcome the lack of prescription and resulting freedom for you to assess the scene for yourself and build your own priorities for policy advice in your own way and time.

A different kind of uncertain ground lies before you when, in whatever way, it is made clear to you that the leader or controlling group (and perhaps other individual members too) have their own instructions or wishes as to what your agenda ought to contain. The permutations of this are endless, especially if you know that in fact there is no overall control or that there are factions or 'hidden agenda' alliances within the formally declared political groupings. All of which may be a permanent feature of life in those authorities which so far have not organised on party political lines. It will be as well to ask yourself why such policies are apparently not overtly declared in the minute book: whether the lobbying is a question of opportunism or testing you out, or whether in fact genuine political power and influence does rest behind what is being said. It may be necessary later to find ways of legitimising or validating policy objectives of this kind, to make sure you are not in fact being asked to risk putting your head above the parapet as a surrogate look-out for someone else – but that kind of problem can be left until you have taken up office.

10. What priorities to give yourself

This question invites you to survey the results of all that you have gleaned from (1) to (9) above to help you set deliberate and positive agendas for your first few days and weeks.

Although they will no doubt overlap and merge into one another, it is likely that you will, consciously or not, want to set yourself ground to cover both for your first few days and for a rather larger distance into whatever introductory or 'honeymoon' period you judge lies ahead. It is as well to think carefully about them both and, as already suggested on page 25, to assert as much control of your diary as you can from the outset.

Planning ahead with your secretary or personal assistant, you can timetable the necessary early introductions or fixed points like council meetings or leader's briefings, but it's wise to leave yourself room for the unexpected. The unexpected may take the form of external emergencies or people coming unannounced to see you whom you will prefer (as a matter of courtesy and favourable impressions) not to turn away if you can avoid doing so. If for no other reason, you need to establish an understanding about things with your secretarial, support or reception staff. How open is your door? How do you and they strike a balance between approachability and overinterruption by matters more sensibly delegated or directed elsewhere? The balance is likely to be a pragmatic one with both sides developing mutual trust and confidence about the right responses.

We return to the subject of the early days in post on pages 31–4.

11. What agendas, minutes, reports, etc. to start seeing regularly

Even in the largest authorities it is tempting to begin by seeing all the flow of committee paper and associated material, even if only as a practice run for a weeding process later. It is a good idea between appointment and taking up position to read yourself into the authority's affairs and it is certainly likely to help you to judge many of the policy and programme priority choices ahead with which this chapter is mainly concerned. Also of course, you can dip and skip as you please with the piles of paper you're likely to be sent – you aren't actually *supposed* to be on top of any of it yet.

Those who haven't been around a chief executive's office previously commonly underestimate both the enormous quantities of paper and propositions that arrive there and the sheer practical problems of trying to be aware of, and keep up-to-date with, all the other departments or divisions at once. Merely to be well informed for its own sake may be worthy but is not much use: the knowledge must be applied to good effect in the overall management of the authority. The more handles you can get from the outset on the flow of paper and the encouragement of useful information, patently the better placed you will be to utilise your time and reading resources optimally later.

12.   How to shape your personal style, management approach and example

Even though many analysts would undoubtedly rate the process of moving to a demanding new job as inherently stressful, there is little doubt either that the adage 'A change is as good as a rest' also has its force, and the prospect of throwing off old problems and taking on new ones can be very refreshing in terms of mental energy and attitude. A clean-sheet move also allows you to make a conscious effort to alter, if not your personality, then at least some elements of its interaction with your way of life.

It can be quite difficult to effect a conscious change of approach or practice in a well-entrenched familiar situation. Granted, however, a new milieu where the established norm is different anyway and that no ready comparison can be made between yesterday and tomorrow, you have a chance to cultivate a different image or approach that you think will help you to carry out your role as chief executive more easily and effectively.

A book like this can give little general advice about a personal style which will be very much your own. On one level your style will be about things like your openness, approachability, evidence of being hardworking and 'in touch', whether you smoke or drink in office hours and if so to what degree, whether you show a liking for expenses, gadgetry or publicity and so on; in other words, attributes with little immediate relevance to provisions in your job description but which will ultimately, perhaps, have rather more to do cumulatively with your overall reputation and others' perception of whether you 'do a good job' (a side issue, maybe, while the going is good but inevitably more significant when it gets tough).

In your new post you presumably want to be healthy and respected as well as surviving and successful, and of course they aren't all the same thing. So it's sensible to review your perception of your own style and try to consider how others (especially others with no preconception of your qualities) are likely to perceive it.

> The newly appointed C.Ex went to a pre-start introductory lunch meeting with his new management team. The treasurer asked him privately and unexpectedly if they were to use his forename or surname. Brought up in a rather formal atmosphere, he opted for surnames on the spur of the moment, but later realised that it had been a mistake – especially with people mainly of similar ages to his own.
>
> Another C.Ex began to keep a weekly time log of hours spent office working, attending civic functions and working at home, as well as weekly units of alcohol consumed (on duty and off) and hours spent on a favoured hobby and relaxation interest he had. Not only were the results revealing and a discipline, they helped him to see trends of fatigue or stress building up gradually which were insufficiently offset by mental and physical recreation.
>
> In a third situation, C.Ex arrived in the authority (in his first C.Ex job) to find a local newspaper headline about him proclaiming 'Axe man cometh'. Such a sensational item, picked up from a previous authority, did not help to get him off to a good start.

Clearly it is particularly important to meet your new colleague directors or chief officers in an informal setting. Being decisive about how to start your job doesn't just mean telling them what you are going to do or want them to do. The early meetings are a good opportunity to ask your new colleagues what they themselves expect from the chief executive and how they see themselves positioned both within the authority and in terms of their own careers. For you, management team involves leading leaders, not followers, and you must recognise that. It is equally important to be the chief executive of all the authority, and not just the central department.

Inextricably linked with your personal style is your management approach. What has already been said about the opportunity to rewrite your personal rules also applies here too, although a genuinely deep-seated change might be much more difficult (if not impossible to achieve).

The weeks before you take up your new post may not afford you much opportunity to disengage from the time pressures of your existing post, but if they do it can be a valuable chance to read and reflect in a way that is generally not possible in a busy daily round. The scope for reading is clearly endless, ranging from large-scale management texts to a brief personal memoir like the SOLACE booklet *Training Needs of the Newly Appointed Chief Executive* (undated).

> Thanks to a six-month notice provision, C.Ex was presented with an unusually long run-up period to his new position, coupled with an in-house

appointment for his successor which allowed him a rare measure of disengagement and selectivity about how he spent his last weeks. He consciously undertook a programme of visits, reading and reflection to take stock of his experiences (and perceived failures and limitations) to date, with a view to establishing his stance in the new authority on a deliberate and properly considered basis.

Your example in this context is not, of course, a paradigm for everyone else to follow – that would be absurd even in a small team, let alone a workforce of several hundred or thousand. The specifics are less important than the clear overall impression generated. It is not in truth very significant whether you are the first to arrive or the last to leave – such claims prove nothing, in themselves. Those around you, however, will know whether you put your time in and work hard. They will tell others. If your commitment is for public consumption only; if your letters of apology are well turned but insincere; if you preach calm but spread the opposite; those around will equally know (and, for that matter, so will you).

13.   How you project your personal image as a new chief executive

Research suggests that first impressions count for more than most of us like to admit. Apparently some 55 per cent of first impressions are based on appearance, 38 per cent on actions (basically body language) and only 7 per cent on content. That means that some 93 per cent of first perceptions are based on non-verbal communication.

This emphasises just how important it is for you, as a chief executive and would-be leader, to project a positive and credible image. Of course, your image goes far beyond appearances – otherwise such an attribute would be seen not only as shallow but probably also as questionable on equal opportunity grounds. But it is important not to neglect the basics.

Perhaps you can think back to examples of impressions you've formed when first encountering supposedly leading people in previous jobs or other contexts. What impressions did they make on you and why? What lessons might you learn and apply to your own case?

The previous pages may seem to present an impossible catalogue of demands for a period of apparent limbo, and also of decisions to be made in a period of widespread ignorance about all the essentials which still lie ahead. They should be read not as a syllabus but rather as a checklist from which you may select at your will. If you recognise your lead-in period for the valuable opportunity it is and use it to good effect in your own eyes, you are unlikely to be anything other than glad once you start work in earnest.

An external non-local government appointment

Much that has been said about other external local government appointees applies equally if you come from outside the service (see pages 19–30). There are, however, some inevitable and important differences if you have not worked in local government previously (or at least do not have substantial recent experience at a fairly senior level, which if you do not will still leave you within the broad definition of this section).

The world of local government is different from the rest of the public sector, let alone the private sector, as well as being very diverse within itself. It is not unique in being different; it is hardly a rare phenomenon to find groups of professionals who believe (no doubt with some justification) that outside their own world the pressures and demands of the job are imperfectly understood. You wouldn't be here if you hadn't already decided that you relished and were ready for the challenges of the local government sector. You should find fellow chief executives uncensorious of your background, willing to share experiences, admiring of your daring and (because they assume you can't really know what's in store) slightly fearful for you. If anything, it's in your early days when you may be able to get away with different attitudes which would raise eyebrows amongst those used to the supposedly traditional ways.

The recent survey referred to on page 19 showed that only about 3 per cent in the period concerned were appointments of chief executives from outside the service, and most of those probably had civil service or health authority backgrounds and so were already well attuned to the public sector. The completely external appointee is therefore entitled to feel somewhat different or special. There is, however, no substantial reason why your job preparation, if you are one of these, need be significantly different.

In one respect, however, it could be useful in speeding up the process of adjustment to the new milieu to spend some time talking to one or two other chief executives who have come by a route similar to that you are now travelling, and who can therefore point you quickly to some of the key areas and issues which you may otherwise take time and unnecessary trouble to discover. These may be much less obvious to the already familiar local government observer and may affect the choices you make about your preparation priorities for day one.

SOLACE will provide contacts who will be willing to help on this basis. It may, anyway, be worth chatting to the local chief executives in the area where you live now. Most chief executives are very willing to share experiences on this sort of basis, and it will help you to build a network of contacts which will be invaluable to you from time to time as your local government career proceeds.

The early days

It would be trite merely to suggest that for, say, your first 100 days you follow the game plan you prepared prior to taking up office. Events will conspire to ensure that there is just enough of the unexpected to waylay your intentions.

Nevertheless, it is important to demonstrate that you are in charge from the outset, able both to challenge and to innovate, and that you can balance – as you will have to do once you are well into the job anyway – what local government tends to call 'the exigencies of the service', with a time-managed methodical approach to what you do personally. In hectic times, you can counter the suggestion that attempting to plan and control is pointless by suggesting that it will only be by retaining a firm grip on whatever you can control that you will stand a chance of retaining the flexibility to deal with the unexpected. Nobody wades successfully across a swirling river without planting their feet as firmly as they can amongst the slippery stones.

You will help yourself to do this not only by keeping your eyes and ears open and listening to what other chief executives have to say about your authority, but by keeping your own counsel sometimes as well. Avoid criticising your pre-decessor directly if you can. If, by implication, your changes of style or approach may be read as critical of what went before, be alive to that and emphasise that you are about to write a fresh page, not correct an old one. And if you are moving from another authority or other job outside, count up how many times you refer to it. What you think of as injecting the new blood of fresh and varied experience is apt to come across as boring 'done it all before' anecdotes to people who until recently thought they were managing perfectly well without you.

A particularly vital aspect of your early tenure, apart from getting to know people within the authority, is the beginning of an external network of community contacts who will help you keep well informed about key elements of local events and activities. Recently a group of newly appointed chief executives, meeting in February 1994, listed (in no particular order) the following organisations or points of contact which for them either had been important in the process of self-introduction and building relationships, or were expected to be so:

- The health authority.
- The TEC (training and enterprise council).
- The police.
- The voluntary sector.
- The regional CBI.
- Parish or community councils.
- Regional government offices.
- The fire authority.
- Development agencies.
- MPs and the MEP.
- Chambers of commerce and trade.
- The urban development corporation.
- The local authority associations.

- Universities and colleges.
- Major local employers.
- Trade unions.
- Local press and media.
- Central government.
- The Local Government Management Board.
- Other associations or groups of local authorities.
- The European dimension.
- Twin towns.
- Major local events.
- Tourist boards.
- Area-related organisations.
- SERPLAN (the South-East Regional Planning Organisation) or its local equivalent.
- Public utilities.
- The National Rivers Authority.
- Military establishments.
- Other local authorities.
- National parks.
- New towns organisations and the Commission for the New Towns.
- Major local developers.
- Local community groups.
- Local pressure groups.
- District or other external auditors.

Clearly this is neither an exhaustive nor a universally applicable list. County or regional chief executives would no doubt include districts, most people would list parish and community councils or residents' groups, and so on. There is no complete or indeed unique answer. But the list, drawn from practical experience in real introductory situations, illustrates the sorts of contacts new chief executives commonly think they need to make to begin to understand and assess the place, role and reputation of their authorities in the areas to which they belong. However easy it would be to become submerged in the internal demands of the new job, time has to be found to 'put yourself about a bit' if you are to determine what perceptions of the authority already exist and where its energies or powers of influence or intervention should be directed. As one participant in the discussion which produced this list put it: 'I tended to meet with the big players.'

However far-sighted your preparation for your new job, full-time actual experience of it is bound to alter your perceptions to some degree. For one thing, you will see the authority much more as a collection of personalities – members and employees alike – than you could do before you started (unless you're an internal appointment, although even there personal relationships may undergo subtle changes, as already discussed on page 19).

As your knowledge of the agenda of the authority develops, along with your knowledge of its people and its problems, so will your ability to categorise your priorities according to the range of chief executive skills which you possess already and those you will acquire and polish as your experience grows. The rest of this book is concerned with different sorts of issues which you may meet in the course of settling down into the job, as the newness wears off and the serious business of being a local authority chief executive really begins.

Chapter 3

The buck stops here

- Isolation
- Loneliness
- Being in the public eye
- Stress
- Stress and pressure
- The chief executive causing stress
- Do I relate to all this?

In Chapter 2 we talked through the period between the moment of being contracted into the new job and a few weeks after you have actually started in the post. We wrote about the conflicting emotions common during those weeks: of pride and elation, of morning-after reality and even of some self-doubt about just how well you can do.

Once you have steered your way through them, what then? This is the point at which, as we said at the end of Chapter 2, 'the serious business of being a local authority chief executive really begins'. Ideally you will reach it after a reasonably planned introductory phase, on your own terms and in a mood of self-confidence (which you need), rather than despondence or arrogance (which you don't). Of course it's unlikely that events will have worked out exactly as you hoped or expected. Probably you've already found out for yourself the truth of the warnings that chief executives must try to be prepared for anything. The way you have responded to these early eventualities will have been an important part of how your reputation has grown; picking up a problem others have left or coping with allegations of someone's misconduct or whatever.

Such experiences may well have brought home to you some of the characteristics or attributes of the job which chief executives always raise when analysing their jobs together. We discuss three of those in this chapter: the isolation, the loneliness, and being in the public eye. Finally we discuss issues around the subject of stress.

Isolation

Those who haven't worked in local government before becoming a chief executive are likely, nonetheless, to have spent time at senior level in some other organisation from which they have had a chance to watch, at close quarters, the style and performance of the person in charge. Those who have been in local government are very likely – particularly if moving directly from a chief officer position – not only to have observed the chief executive in the ordinary way but also to have been part of an overtly interrelated and interdependent team of officers. That 'corporate comfort' factor is likely to be absent from the outlook of a chief executive.

True, it may be present in a different form: the support given by others will be very important to everyone. The key difference, and the reason for the isolation, is that in the last resort the chief executive cannot just regard him or herself as part of a team. Whether you like it or not, to be head of the paid service is to be set apart from the rest of the employees: set apart by statute (section 4 of the Local Government and Housing Act 1989); by the elected members; by the rest of the employees; and not least probably by the public.

The reality simply is that as chief executive you are a different kind of employee from everyone else. The staffing and 'proper management' duties of section 4 of the 1989 Act are upon your shoulders, and even though such responsibilities can of course be greatly eased *by* others they cannot be shared *with* others. This statement of the apparently obvious may seem trite, but experience of talking to groups of new chief executives over several years convinces us that the actuality of this sense of difference is frequently underestimated on appointment. It is often drawn out some months into the job as one of the immediate personal verdicts on 'How was it for me?' In other words, people frequently find that the isolation of the job takes more getting used to than they expected.

Everyone will experience it differently, so can we capture and pin down the elusive sense of what we mean by isolation? Physically you are likely to be surrounded by attention of all kinds: personal staff, incoming telephone calls, faxes and ordinary mail, people who want or expect to see you, and more committees, commitments and engagements than you can sensibly handle. To other people you probably don't look very isolated at all.

This kind of isolation has little or nothing to do with appearances. Looking back on their promotion or appointment, chief executives mostly come to accept that they made a quantum leap in moving from a very senior management position to the ultimate management position. No amount of training can disguise a pilot's first solo flight. No amount of rehearsals can quite equate to the feeling of playing before a live audience. The sensation that 'it's all down to me' in a real situation cannot quite be reached before you actually have it.

We can refer again to those unexpected crises or turns of events that almost certainly have already arisen during your early weeks. These are important to your emerging reputation. They are equally as important to your own self-confidence because of the realisation they can bring home to you: that this sort of thing is what you are for and why you are paid more than everybody else.

It is your decision, your judgement on the line, your can to carry however wisely someone else is advising you to act. The buck has stopped here!

However the realisation comes to them, most chief executives do not find this necessarily a disturbing or difficult experience: rather they find it stimulating as a reinforcement of the status and role to which they have long aspired. However closely you may have worked with other chief executives and shared opinions on key decisions or situations, the extent to which they felt the burden of final personal responsibilities is unlikely to have been clear to you. There will no doubt be times when you are urged by others to take a particular course of action and will think to yourself (while thanking them politely for that contribution and helping you make up your mind) '*You* don't have to go away and actually *do* what you've just suggested *I* do!'

Experiencing isolation may give rise to a sense of loneliness, as the two are so often linked. In the next section we consider the loneliness aspect and also how the job characteristic of isolation can be approached so as to reduce its dangers.

Loneliness

While things are going well it is not difficult to relish a position that appears to give you unique advantages in being at the apex of a complex organisation while able to call upon the collective skills and energies of many other people with whom you describe yourself as a team. In a complex organisation, however, the many parts are likely to be in many different states at the same time. And, in today's situation of unending re-invention and challenge for local government, you are rarely going to get beyond cautious optimism about the overall picture. How will you be affected by all these unending demands? We talk of the pressures of the pace of events under the heading of 'stress' on pages 43–4, but although the dividing lines are never that sharp, this section is primarily about the problems that being on the end of any line are likely to pose.

The average employee is likely to have access to at least three levels of comment and discussion to provide outlets for their views. At work there is a formal level: the sort of things people say to their superiors, often in quite formal language, feeling themselves 'on the record'. There is also what they say to their own trusted friend or peer group: their contribution to the 'canteen culture'. This is likely to be considerably different from the 'official' version. Third, at home they may share different opinions, different topics, different degrees of confidentiality again; and of course they may have a variety of other outlets combining changing elements of all of these depending on who else is listening and the (small p) personal political context of the conversation. It is easy to see how a remark like 'It's going to be difficult to save ten per cent on our budget' said to a superior can become 'They're going to have to lose staff' in the general office gossip and 'I think I'm going to be made redundant' back at home.

As chief executive you have one fewer level, or outlet, of this kind than others in the authority. Even the rest of the management team can talk together about you. You, however, have no one with whom certain types of confidence can be shared (and hence to some degree unburdened) who is either of equivalent status or senior to you. It is likely, too, that you are cut off from the office grapevine to which nearly everyone else is privy (this may affect other very senior people and one or two of your own personal staff as well).

C.Ex had a personal assistant whose relationship with another employee was well known to everyone else but him. Moving amongst his immediate staff daily, he was effectively denied the gossips and rumour exchanged as a matter of course in any social grouping of that kind.

Another C.Ex situation of this sort involved informal office circulation of a pamphlet alleging fault in the very sensitive and difficult handling of a matter which had led to tragedy. The C.Ex was not aware of it until a copy was provided for his secretary, presumably on the basis that she would ensure that he did come to know of it without being directly contacted.

This last situation can sometimes pose dilemmas for your close personal staff too. Working with everyday access to you and your office and reading (even filtering) a large part of your personal correspondence, calls and visitors, they also have probably set themselves some way apart from the common office politics. They have to balance any disadvantages of their seemingly ambivalent position with the satisfaction of being in the know, close to the centre of things and likely to be firmly identified around the authority with your reputation.

How do chief executives report their sense of loneliness? Not all would use that word, of course, but in discussions around this topic it emerges as a regular choice to express the sense in which postholders experience the problems and inhibitions of not being able openly, frankly or fully to discuss some issues at work.

Why might you feel inhibited? Some of the many reasons include the following, in no particular order:

1. You feel the subject is too confidential for you to risk it getting out.
2. The people you would ordinarily go to are themselves part of the problem or the range of issues you are considering, so they clearly can't be approached.
3. You don't trust or value the advice or contribution you would probably get.
4. The subject is too personal because your own reputation, performance or image is somewhat at stake, and you do not want to reveal (or be assumed to have signalled) self-doubt, anxiety or weakness.
5. You have confidence in the position you've reached within yourself and either don't need it being knocked now or consider that no one else has really had the overview from which you've made up your mind.

6. Your predecessor never consulted much and it's expected you will know what to do and just get on with it.
7. An undertaking or expectation of confidentiality has been imposed on you by an elected member or political group which you must keep not just in spirit but also literally.
8. The office system frankly leaks like a sieve and you don't know who you can trust or whether in fact you can trust anyone.
9. There isn't time to talk to the people of your choice for some reason.
10. You could speak confidentially and it would no doubt be respected but your instinct or inclinations tell you it's better not to do so.

The 10 reasons above (and permutations of them) are all workplace-based. They may well not inhibit conversations at home or even outside the office locally. Yet clearly even here there are limitations. No one who shares your home, however sympathetic and willing they are to take your side, perhaps has the experience of managing a large organisation or knows your people and problems sufficiently well to be of real help. There is the added danger of breach of confidentiality if you let slip unguarded remarks in any other context where they may get back and cause you embarrassment later.

It has to be emphasised that there is nothing unusual in feeling closed in by a problem (or even a range of them), and that it needn't be taken as a sign of inadequacy that you aren't immediately convinced of the right thing to do and persuaded in your own mind that there is no alternative. It can safely be said that *all* chief executives, even the most experienced, most outwardly calm, most apparently dogmatic, have doubts from time to time about the wisest course of action or whether they can 'get through the members' what (given a free hand) they would like to do. And there are plenty of problems or issues to which there is no single correct answer, no right box to tick, no perfect mixture of advantages without unwanted drawbacks.

These are the situations that require your experience, your judgement, and something which is unique to you within your authority: your perspective as chief executive.

The single most effective way – in fact for most people virtually the only way – to combat the problems of loneliness at the top and isolation (to go back to pages 35–7) is to begin as soon as possible after you've been appointed to develop contacts with chief executive colleagues in other authorities. Except by chance, they are unlikely to have a detailed knowledge of your area or the key members and officers of your authority. This matters little: in fact it is often an advantage because they can have an objectivity which is difficult for you and they may tell you to ask questions you had not thought to pose to yourself. Perhaps in a strange way it may help them to release their own problems. (We also comment about mentoring and action-learning in Chapter 6.)

Getting to know a variety of colleagues – through SOLACE, or through association, county or other meetings or conferences – will soon provide a ready store of people who operate in the same sort of local government world as you do. They may lack your local database but they speak your language in other ways through the medium of their own experience. Like you they cope with leaders, auditors, ombudsmen or recalcitrant colleagues, and they can listen with a sympathy and empathy others cannot provide. They can also advise from a pragmatic point of view that doesn't ignore the realities of what you can expect to achieve.

You may in fact find that hearing yourself argue and defend your point of view has already served to convince you in your own mind of whatever you began by proposing. If this happens, you will recognise it as an important contribution. It is in fact a contribution which, for the kinds of reasons discussed earlier in this section, you very probably could not get within the confines of your own authority because of your unique, isolated and often rather lonely position.

Being in the public eye

This is sometimes also called 'dealing with public scrutiny'. You will have some idea even before you apply for a particular post whether it is likely that the chief executive will have, or be expected to have, a high profile within the authority and its area.

It won't necessarily be the case that a big city post involves more publicity and media exposure than a rural-based authority post spread over two or three small towns: the priorities of local editors and your own public relations output will play a big part. Nevertheless there will be some obvious tendencies and, assuming you aren't already working in the area, you should take care to find out about them as soon as possible.

For one thing, there will be the danger (referred to on page 22) of being asked for public comment on key local issues before you can possibly be properly briefed and guarded about them. But you can expect some coverage of your appointment and will probably welcome it as a way of first introductions being made to your name and prospective arrival. Important as the media are for you, there is more than the media to being in the public eye. For one thing, there is the question of council expectations about what sort of profile you should try to have. Do they expect you to be well known, in fact a community leader, or is that a role they think local politicians should play? We discuss this further on pages 98–9.

There is also the question of how you, and to a degree any partner or family you have, are going to react to being regarded at times by the media as 'fair game'. This is yet one more thing on which you will find it an advantage to have a considered and positive attitude.

It goes without saying that you are by law politically restricted by section 2 of the Local Government and Housing Act 1989 and must reflect an impartial or neutral political outlook. That applies, of course, to most senior local government officers as well as chief executives. For any chief executive, however, even more than for other chief and senior officers, the requirements of section 2 (which only served to confirm the almost universal practice of past years) are only a limited part of the expectations.

Like anyone else, you are entitled to your privacy and your own free time. In practice the requirements will encroach on both of these. Because of the possibility of emergencies or out-of-hours contacts, you are never quite beyond the reach of duty at any time unless you are well away from your authority's area. Even then, actions which your authority consider incompatible with their expectations of you will be very serious for their continued confidence in you.

That is looking on the down side. Much more likely is that you suffer the same drawbacks of your position that most chief executives probably experience. You can't be sure when or if you're recognised. You are likely to have to put up with endless small talk stories about alleged council atrocities of one sort or another and barbs about how much better life would be if you, the members or your employees weren't the dunderheads they've supposedly proved themselves to be. You may have children who tend to be referred to at school as 'the chief executive's children', implying that somehow they are wealthier and posher than the rest of the children or who are singled out in even more unpleasant ways.

C.Ex was playing at the local tennis club. A chance remark having revealed his job, he was regaled with a problem about someone's wish to fell a protected tree on a site too close to his own home for comfort. The officers involved, against whom idiocy was alleged, later proved to have acted quite properly and politely. Relaxation was switched into official response, and after being told for the third time that 'I'll shut up when I've said this', C.Ex found himself amidst a potentially awkward conflict of personal and public activities. Two days later, another club member telephoned him at home for more planning advice on another issue.

That anecdote illustrates that you are never quite off duty, at least in your own area. People who do not set out necessarily to be compromising may not realise how you are bound to react when confronted with an issue on which you have or could have an official position or have to be politically neutral.

You can do little about this. It pays to be diplomatic, even when for you this is clearly neither the time nor the place. Most chief executives learn to guard their privacy as best they may and can take part in one of the endless council-bashing conversations without becoming too seriously involved or affected by it. It's an aspect of your job. You can't change it, so learn to live with it.

It's one thing for you to accept that your privacy or freedom of action is affected somewhat by your position. You may well see it as no great problem most of the time, and in any event you have voluntarily exchanged it for the status, salary, satisfaction and even perhaps power of your position. What about any other home effects of being in the public eye?

There are many people whose partners or family members would argue that these days there is no particular social position or exposure attached to your job anyway. For some, any community or social role – going to civic and other local functions and the like – may indeed be minimal. There are, again, some who do experience that element but either enjoy it or don't mind it. But there are some who find the expectations of them both demanding in time and cost terms, and even onerous.

It has to be said that the anecdotal evidence available to us suggests, rightly or wrongly, that the expectations of partners of male chief executives are different from or greater than those of partners of female chief executives. This no doubt has much to do with the way things actually are, rather than the way you may perhaps think they ought to be.

Increasingly partners of male chief executives are coming together when opportunities allow them to discuss what they find those expectations to be and how they cope with them according to experience, whether they are employed in some way themselves, have young children at home or whatever.

This is true too in the USA, where political correctness has not prevented partners facing dilemmas like these meeting on common ground at International City/County Management Association (ICMA) activities and conferences to discuss what some of them evidently regarded as a kind of unpaid personal/secretarial role combined with an obligation to 'look the part' (whatever that means) on required occasions. For many who earn their living in areas like the local property market or work for would-be council contractors, additional areas of ethical difficulty (and indeed grave potential embarrassment for the chief executive personally) open up.

What can we usefully say about such issues as these? There are as many variations of them as there are partnerships, characters and contexts. Probably the best advice is to talk through the issues and not to assume, for example, that a partner can feel as comfortable as maybe you can with your politically restricted status. If you are not to be compromised, however unfairly, your partner's own views may have to be unarticulated. You in turn may have to be positive about limiting the effects of some of the demands on you in terms of the way they could affect your partner.

It would be wise, at the outset, to talk frankly with your authority about any particular problems in this latter area, so that you don't mislead or perhaps initially work too hard to do so many functions and activities that inevitably you, or both of you, can't keep it up and run the risk of being stigmatised later as having lost interest.

But if your partner has a busy career of their own or you have a partner who is an invalid or you both share in the demands of a young family, it's best to let this be known at once (it may even be discernible from your application in some cases). That way everyone knows where they are and if this is an authority with civic or out-of-hours commitments inconsistent with what you are able or want to offer, it is better to be honest about that at the outset because, otherwise neither side will be finding what they are looking for.

We refer specifically to church-going on pages 89–90 and, in general terms, to the very broad issue of ethics and ethical dilemmas on page 86.

Stress

The phenomenon of stress is much better understood than it was. Yet the word itself is used so much, and in so many different contexts, that it is in danger of becoming completely debased and in the famous phrase 'signifying nothing'. In common parlance it seems to have acquired an overtone of anxiety which a phrase of yesterday like 'nerves' did not apparently possess.

Obviously it is not in itself a phenomenon confined to chief executives. It can be experienced by all employees (quite apart from its occurrence outside the work place) but as the generic word becomes more accurately recognised as a handy label for a wide variety of circumstances and symptoms, it has become increasingly appreciated that managers as a class are particularly vulnerable. In different ways, making unpopular decisions and implementing them can be just as stressful as being on the receiving end of them.

Although a few common-sense points and principles are likely to be perceived by nearly everyone, stress as a medical or psychological condition is not an area for homespun philosophy. Properly experienced and trained advice is essential. This section therefore confines itself to process rather than prescription.

You applied for the job originally in the confidence that you could tackle it well if given the chance. Indeed, it would have been pardonable self-confidence, rather than arrogance, to come to the interview in the frame of mind that you were indeed literally the best candidate for the job. Later you will need resilience, stamina and overall good health to give your best in a position which will ask a lot of your time, your patience, your tact, your energy: in short, of all your characteristics and capabilities.

Remember that all the runners are fresh at the start of a course and that even the winner is tired at the end. Assess yourself against the demands to be made, and make time for the simple health screening checks that are easily available nowadays. Take a little time to get yourself advice on how to recognise danger signals in yourself and do something about them. There are some useful books around like *Pressure at Work: A survival guide* by Tanya Arroba and Kim James (McGraw-Hill, 1987). The habits of work you get into as you settle into being a chief executive may be hard to change later.

It is often surprisingly difficult to know just exactly how much time you do put in. Both the writers of this book keep informal personal records of hours at work and other details. We do it differently. One of us records a breakdown of office, committee, social and work-at-home hours put in as chief executive. The other pays particular attention also to units of alcohol consumed and time devoted to an important leisure pursuit. How you do it hardly matters, but even a rough check will give you revealing information about trends in your work pattern which you may otherwise not notice or not properly appreciate. Both of us, incidentally, define as 'work' anything which, were we not chief executives in those particular jobs, we would not be doing. It may be social, it may be enjoyable, but you're on duty and carrying certain responsibilities with you, so it's fair to count it in.

Page 94 of Alan Norton's 1991 INLOGOV study into *The Role of Chief Executive in British Local Government: Its origins and development, present reality and future* provides a table of average hours chief executives recorded themselves as working in a typical week. A response of 256 yielded an overall average of some 52 hours, the parameters of average variation being about 57 hours for those in London boroughs and about 46 for those in Scottish districts.

Stress and pressure

There is a story of someone asking a chief executive whether they thought they could comfortably handle three things at once, and getting the answer no. 'Why not?' pursues the questioner. 'Well,' comes the response, 'for a chief executive there wouldn't be enough going on.'

Interestingly the book by Tanya Arroba and Kim James referred to in the last section was called *Pressure* – not *Stress* – *at Work*. On page 3, the authors define the difference between the two concepts as follows: '*Pressure is the aggregate of all the demands placed on you* – physical, environmental and psychological. On the other hand, *stress is your response to an inappropriate level of pressure*. It is response to pressure, not the pressure itself.'

The authors go on to illustrate this key distinction. No doubt we will all be able to recall incidents where events, for us, were stimulating and brought out our best performance, and others where we were rendered anxious or fretful and somehow cornered by events. An incident which induces A's optimum response may easily induce the opposite in B. A may finish the day tired out but satisfied, B exhausted and with lowered self-esteem.

It is as well to recognise basic symptoms in yourself as a matter of common sense. If the kinds of issues discussed in the earlier parts of this chapter – about the isolation and loneliness of the job and tendency to be in the local public eye – are causing you problems, your network links with other chief executives may be particularly valuable to ease pressure and hold stress at bay, even if a professional response cannot in itself be a substitute for a medical one should that need ever arise.

The chief executive causing stress

Deprived as you may be of some of the everyday give-and-take of the office round, it can be even more difficult than usual to see yourself as others see you. You should not underestimate your capacity to cause pressure and stress in those around you and, indeed, in the authority in general.

This could arise in a variety of ways. Here are 10 possible examples:

1. You may not properly appreciate some situation about which you convey instructions, so causing the recipient to feel under an obligation to meet unrealistic requirements or to avoid an outcome which it is known you do not in fact intend.
2. You may cut across some actual or perceived seniority by going directly to employee B, for some reason, which bypasses employee A and unwittingly hurts A (perhaps perceived as a signal that you do not trust A or wish A to be sidelined in some way).
3. You may give an instruction which your subordinates think is ill-advised, and have not been able to accept in some way through consultation or discussion.
4. What you put as a straightforward request may be interpreted as a need for much more work/information/performance than you intended.
5. Your requests may be incorrectly transmitted through intermediaries with unintended and unpredictable results.
6. You may have heavier boots than you like to think (you try to be informal, but they respect your position too much to be relaxed in your presence and behave uneasily or unnaturally as a result).
7. Your style involves a lot of use of bustle, nervous energy, and rushing from one thing to another, conveying an example and atmosphere of tension rather than calm.
8. Others – and even perhaps members – contradict you when you aren't there, posing dilemmas for those trying to do the right thing by everyone.
9. You are known to be having a tough time generally, so that those who depend on you personally in some sense become insecure themselves.
10. People find you difficult to work with for some reason.

Let's hope 8–10 never arise, and instead take two trivial, but real, examples of 6, the 'big boots' syndrome.

C.Ex regularly passed a photocopier en route to his office. A very young trainee was struggling with the paper-feed, and he made a light-hearted remark about how frequently they had trouble with that machine. Later he was told that the trainee had interpreted his speaking in such circumstances as criticism or rebuke and had been very upset. He was also told that to say anything later about the incident would be unlikely to have the mollifying result intended because the trainee concerned was quite simply afraid of him.

Another C.Ex told how, in his early days, he saw through a window someone who was coming to see him stop and turn away. On enquiring, he found his secretary had intercepted and dismissed his caller because she considered the caller inappropriately dressed by customary local rules to call on the chief executive. The would-be caller had no tie on.

This anecdote sets out just how easy it is for a chief executive, who no doubt hopes to earn respect but would be appalled at the idea of inducing fear, to misread the responses of people round about. They take notice of the aura of chief executive authority, real or imagined, which the unadorned individual plainly does not possess.

There is no way to avoid this dilemma except to tread carefully, to try to gauge reactions from others' points of view and think how you would have responded yourself in such a situation when you were relatively new or junior. You may like to think your style today is less autocratic and more consensual but if people are meeting you infrequently or for the first time, and the aura of your predecessors in post travels before you, will they know how relaxed and informal you like to think you are? They can't be blamed if they err on the side of caution.

Especially in a larger authority, you are unlikely ever to get to know everyone well enough to feel you have entirely solved the problems of untypical or unnatural behaviour. There will always be people who tense up if you are around, who inhibit their strength of feeling, say what they think you want to hear or behave diffidently and convey a misleading body language message to you. Another side of the 'big boots' syndrome is the 'chocolate biscuits' syndrome: you routinely visit a department and they turn it into a special occasion (it perhaps *is* a special occasion of a kind for them); or you visit unannounced, priding yourself on 'walking the job', and out of earshot they're asking 'What's he/she here for?' and starting rumours of bad news.

The only way to keep such visits routine in impact is genuinely to keep making them routinely, so that from their own experience people know that your arrival is not the harbinger of bad news.

A great deal has been written about style and example in leadership. It is so obvious that juniors observe how seniors behave that it doesn't require elaborating. Nevertheless it is important to think through the real nature of the example you want to set. People's working hours and styles are different and it would be foolish to expect conformity in areas of behaviour where individuality is not only a strength but a practical necessity. In any event, people are more likely to respect rules they know you have to make – to meet safety standards, or comply with the law, for instance – if you avoid making rules you don't have to make.

What kind of an example is it to be first in to work every morning? By definition, *nobody else can do that*. Many people have probably got flexible working hours anyway from which both they and the authority benefit. By all means set an example of putting your time in giving hard work and productive output: they mean more, and the employees around you will know whether or not you pull your weight regardless of whether or not you regularly disconnect the burglar alarm. Be a workaholic and most employees again will be discouraged. They can't or don't want to be like that and if that's what it takes to win your approval they probably won't try. Moving to a new authority, or even to a new job within the same authority, gives you an excellent opportunity for changing or modifying your own work habits or style without anybody really noticing you've done it.

Do I relate to all this?

In this chapter we've tried to point out and exemplify some of the characteristics of being a chief executive and some of the issues of mental stress and resilience which regularly emerge as people discuss the process of their work as chief executives. You may feel that none of it really applies to you. That's fine. Or if it does apply that, as the advertisement used to say, you don't suffer from it. That's fine, too.

We are not saying 'This can be an isolated and lonely job, therefore you *will* feel isolated and lonely and it *will* get you down'. What we *are* saying is 'This can be an isolated and lonely job, you *may* be conscious of such feelings from time to time or over particular issues'. We think you may have wanted to become a chief executive in the first place, at least in part, because of the challenge and thrill to be obtained from being out there in the no. 1 spot. The moments when the responsibilities are heaviest for you may be stimulating, even exhilarating, rather than depressing or demotivating.

The perceptions of these characteristics or attributes of the chief executive post are common: your reaction to it will be varied and individual (probably unique as we are so different). When at times an outlet or discussion outside the authority can be useful or underpin your own made-up mind, your SOLACE colleagues will recognise the characteristics too. They will know where you are coming from, what the grist and grain of the job are about and very likely can both sympathise and empathise constructively. You can turn back to your workplace with renewed self-confidence which will be as visible to others as you are conscious of it yourself.

All that is good for both mental and physical health and strength, which any chief executive needs. It *can* be a tough job. As you go on, you will learn how to carry the load in the most effective way for *you*, and how better to appreciate the impact you have, in turn, on those around you who have to work with you.

Chapter 4

It's relationships that matter

- The range of relationships
- The political leaderships
- The chief officers
- Employees generally
- The trade unions, the press and other key relationships

You won't read management books and articles for very long before you come across somebody's quote to the effect that basically only people matter in any organisation. Systems and buildings, resources and equipment, neat charts and export orders, and whatever else you care to mention, don't of themselves design, build, sell, or maintain anything. You know yourself in what sense those statements are true. They are a salutary reminder that even if we are emerging from it, we are still not entirely out of an era when we (employers in general) failed to attach enough importance to the individual qualities and contribution that could come from all our employees. (Their rights and status too were often neglected, but we put the contributory qualities first here because those emphasise most of all what was often missing.)

Of course, you also know in what sense the 'people are absolutely everything' epithets exaggerate to make the point. These miracle-worker employees will need (indeed will *deserve*) a variety of other requirements to be right as prerequisites to a success story: they need resources and external circumstances to be in at least a minimum state to allow them to begin to deliver any part of their potential. Nevertheless, however you view the interrelated parts of the constituency you govern as chief executive, you are overwhelmingly likely to conclude that putting people first, and a long way first, on your list of priorities is the right thing to do.

But it isn't enough just to pin a notice on your office door to say 'I put people first here'. In any event, that kind of gesture is apt to sound like transatlantic tokenism and is equally apt to bounce back on you. Which way are you going to look when events present you with a list of redundancies in the very same week the authority signs a new contract for some expensive hardware?

If you are not to become a prisoner of your own precepts, publicly setting up unrealistic standards for yourself, you need to have worked out a more fully rounded approach to the complex issues surrounding the deceptively simple word *people*. That is why we have set aside this chapter to concentrate on *relationships*. Their importance to your very survival in post cannot be underestimated, and you will need to be systematic about them.

The range of relationships

First of all, a kind of exercise. You have an assessment, a mental picture, of your new authority. In particular you have some idea of its strengths, and probably a better idea of its weaknesses: the areas you think you'll be spending significant time on trying to improve. The authority did not come to be like that by spontaneous creation. It probably evolved over a long period of time, the product of past administrations, employees and circumstances all of which have combined to make it the way it is. The correlation between where previous efforts have been concentrated and what you think is now done well may not be all that good. Assume for a moment that the way the authority and all its constituent parts are now is deliberate, and exactly as you would have wanted them to be (not true, almost certainly, but try to imagine it). Now – and this is the exercising part – try to imagine all that would have been necessary deliberately to produce the picture and product that you see today. We think you will find it surprisingly difficult, such would be the range of attitudes and eventualities that you would have to have assembled all at once and focused on the same point in time.

What is the point of such an absurd flight of fancy? Actually there are two points. The first is that you have set out for yourself the *inertia of the authority*, the ongoing state it is currently in and which is the derivative or residual product of all that has gone before. Whatever choices have been made in the past about training priorities, political priorities, cuts, allocations and the like, their influence has been felt and assimilated by the organisation as a whole, but the organisation has continued to roll forward under its own momentum. Any organisation of three people or more – let alone several hundred or thousand people – has a tendency to self-generate a life of its own – or how else would we say that any team or group could become greater than the sum of its parts?

The second point of this mental exercise is that it is likely to have provided a roll-call of people, and hence relationships, which you will have to visit or form to stand any real chance of changing the organisation in the way you want to. Not much will happen merely because you say so (probably *nothing* in the world of employee *attitudes* just because you say so), so you are going to have to get out there to *influence* and *persuade*.

At this point you may like to look back to pages 32–3 in Chapter 2 to remind yourself of the catalogue of local contacts or organisations which was seen as relevant by a group of new chief executives. Not all of them were relevant for everyone but most people related to a lot of them. In the remainder of this chapter we talk in more detail about a few of the key headings or categories which for most people will be particularly important: part of what Professor Janice Morphet in her book *The Role of Chief Executives in Local Government* (Longman, 1993) calls 'chief executives within the town hall'.

That doesn't mean that we can in fact presume or describe your main priorities for you – you have to do that. The rules here are the same as in the rest of this book: have the confidence to be different if your own experience and instincts tell you to be. In paragraph 2.10 of the *Report of the Working Party on the Internal Management of Local Authorities in England* entitled *Community Leadership and Representation: Unlocking the potential* (HMSO, July 1993) the working party conclude that they 'deliberately do not identify an ideal internal management model and recommend its application as a blueprint to all authorities'. They also 'recognise that different approaches will be appropriate for different authorities, and that it is for them and not central government to choose which arrangements to adopt'. At the same time, we think some at least of the following observations, based on our exchanges with others over the years, may be helpful. After the specific categories we include a short general heading about some of the many other relationships that go to form part of your network of professional dealings.

The political leaderships

Legislation took little or no account of party political realities before 1985. Since that start (see section 33 of the Local Government Act 1985 about membership of joint committees following abolition of the metropolitan counties and the GLC) statute has ventured into the area in a number of ways. Probably the most notable are the political party proportionality rules of section 15 of the Local Government and Housing Act 1989, the political restriction of officers under section 2 of the same Act, and section 2 of the Local Government Act 1986 restraining political party publicity financed by local government funds.

For chief executives, local politics and their own relationship to them have long been at the very nub of the job. With very few exceptions (and those mostly discreet) chief executives and their predecessors in title have been, in modern times at least, politically impartial by common expectation and assumption. In that sense the 1989 Act seemingly made *de jure* what was already widely the case *de facto*. In other words, the practical significance for most chief executives personally of a law which applied to them all was extremely limited.

That practical significance instead lay in their relationship with the various – and presumably competing – local political leaderships within that authority with whom they had to work. In this section we categorise those groupings as council leader, opposition leader, other party leaders, controlling group, opposition groups, and independents. We consider each of these six in turn.

Leader of the council

There is no legal requirement for councils to have a leader though it has been common for many years, as party politics has played a wider role in local government generally, for the councillors who comprise the controlling group to elect one of their number to be the political leader of the council. Though a well-recognised role, it will normally be quite separate from the chairman or (lord) mayor of the council who is that authority's civic head. In terms of civic precedence the leader is formally entitled to no particular status or formality over other elected members at large, though recognition of some kind may be afforded informally by local custom or pragmatism.

For many, if not most, chief executives their relationship with the leader will inevitably be the principal factor not only in their ordinary working week but also in their success and, indeed, often in their very survival in post. Self-evidently it is a relationship to be thought about, consciously worked at, yet not developed into overdependence or familiarity.

While some leaders and chief executives will consciously sit down together to agree guidelines on how they plan to meet, brief each other and so on, for others a deliberate effort of this sort will be unnecessary. For others again, the leader may simply seek to spell out how things are going to be, leaving the chief executive little practical choice but to agree.

If the council leader has an office in the building and occupies it extensively, it does not necessarily follow that the chief executive is overshadowed. A powerful alliance may develop based on the regularity of contact and the depth of mutual understanding, or 'reading', which can be achieved. Clearly the size of the authority and the political majority in question will influence this chemistry (or should it be alchemy?) as will the personalities and external circumstances of the people involved.

It is a common characteristic of the groupings listed here that as chief executive you cannot choose them (though *they* may to varying degrees have chosen *you*) and so must take them as you find them. The 'arranged marriage' aspect of this has to be accepted, with its element of chance about how much or how little the constituent people are naturally ill at ease in their dealings with each other.

Nevertheless, the chief executive's relationship with the leader of the council cannot be just a 'that's the way it is, take it or leave it' affair. In the following paragraphs we postulate some considerations which may inform some of the thinking behind the deliberate approaches chief executives may put into working at their relationship with their leader.

First, are there any formal requirements, laid down by standing orders, council resolutions or other local custom and practice? And if so, are they lawful and/or transferable or applicable to the changed circumstances of your appointment rather than that of your predecessor?

It is not unreasonable that the council, which has decided to have someone in the position of leader, should have provided a number of special arrangements – in addition, of course, to the special responsibility allowance which was probably paid in the past under section 177A of the Local Government Act 1972. Possibly the leader has not only an office and the usual accoutrements of notepaper and computer terminal, etc. but even political assistants appointed under section 9 of the Local Government and Housing Act 1989. The leader will expect a special degree of briefing and access to officers (and indeed priority in those) over and above other councillors.

Secondly, people unfamiliar with the ways of local government politics often ask how it is possible to equate the principle of the chief executive (like others) being the servant of the whole council with the reality that certain councillors (leaders, chairs, members of a controlling group, etc.) expect and get treatment according to an apparently different set of ground rules. Since the 1989 Act most of these realities are strictly or explicitly recognised by statute (though the position of leader has not yet, we think, received a specific mention in any statute paragraph 8 of the Local Government (Committees and Political Groups) Regulations 1990, S.I. No. 1553, comes as close as makes little difference).

Our explanation of this apparent paradox or contradiction is this: the chief executive is the employee of the council, rather than of the councillors either individually or collectively in any way. In law, the council is an entity, legally distinct from even the sum total of all the councillors together.

The council can only express its will, ultimately, at the decision of the majority. A majority vote in a properly called and constituted meeting becomes (unless there is invalidity or unlawfulness for some external reason) a legally effective decision. It is axiomatic that in this respect the chief executive, by acting on such a decision, in effect carries out the wishes of some councillors but not others.

In practical terms, however, the corporation of the council is a legal fiction, but the councillors themselves are real. Are they not all entitled to equal treatment?

The answer to this, we believe, is *yes* so far as the law requires them all to be the same, but *no* so far as it allows the council to decide differently as a result of the way it orders its affairs. To quote an example, attendance allowances allow certain councillors who fall within the prescribed class to receive an additional kind of payment. Similarly, the chief executive must treat all councillors equally so far as matters pertaining to their general council memberships, rights and duties are concerned, but also must respect what we term *the political realities* prescribed by the decisions the council has made about how it will conduct its affairs. Those decisions, whether or not motivated at root by party political loyalties, will have been reflected in appointments of chairs of committees and all sorts of other working practices.

The particular dilemmas of how those political realities may affect practices like the giving or withholding of briefings or information are referred to further on: see page 54. We return here directly to the particular example of political reality for most chief executives, the leader of the council, and the third of our considerations.

Thirdly, what ideally should be the tenor of your relationship as chief executive with the council leader? We emphasise here *your* relationship with *him* or *her*, since it is much more difficult obviously for you to influence matters the opposite way round.

In our view the ideal is to achieve confidence without personal compromise, trust without dependency, cordiality without familiarity, and informality without casualness. In other words, don't get too close: don't be so closely identified that a change of leader inevitably raises the presumption of a possible need for a change of chief executive. Friendliness is one thing, friendship another.

In discussions with groups of chief executives, a change of leader, irrespective of change or not of party with it, is frequently singled out as a key event for a chief executive. The previous relationship goes and has to be reformed in circumstances which, if the previous leader has gone for political rather than personal or external reasons, can be fraught with difficulty for the remaining half of yesterday's duo. We return to the question of relationships with members generally in this context on pages 55–7.

Fourthly, is 'the leader' actually more than one person, or the key person politically to whom you must relate? It may be that there is a small inner circle of members who effectively provide a collective leadership, or else that someone other than the nominal leader is generally recognised to be the key figure of political authority. Or there may be a 'leader's group', the kind of arrangement described as possessed by councils C and D on pages 22 and 24 of the 1993 report on internal management referred to above on page 50.

This is bound to muddy the waters a little and make more complex the web of relationships you have to weave and maintain appropriately. It probably will not, however, produce a result much different from what the rest of this section is about: the need to forge and maintain a tenable, stable and hopefully unpatronising and uncompromising working relationship with wherever political power and influence in your authority ultimately lie.

Forming this sort of relationship may be quite difficult at the best of times, but suppose that the leader is not 'all right' and is part of the problem? Suppose that you (and perhaps others), far from accepting the leader as morally upright, regard him or her as morally corrupt with the position of leader being abused? Suppose there are other problems which have weakened the leader's position, or there is a drink problem or an investigation or something which inhibits the nature of the relationship you can form?

This is perhaps a general point since obviously leaders aren't unique in these respects. There are people who we consider 'play games' by apparently having a hidden agenda, who are difficult seemingly for the sake of it, who delight in sowing discord and mistrust or deliberately say the opposite of what they really mean for reasons of their own. Situations like these present particular dilemmas which the direct approach of conventional assertiveness is unlikely to resolve easily. You have to accept the council's choice of leader. You have to accord whatever courtesies and privileges attach to that role in your authority. But you can temper this with greater reserve than you might otherwise show. We discuss this issue of space between you and your leader more on page 91 in Chapter 7. What you have noticed has probably been noticed by others as well. That may mean that this difficulty will solve itself for you, since you can probably only improve matters for yourself to a limited degree. It will probably make you more 'correct', more formal, more inclined to cover yourself in writing and so on. At least if you recognise the motives and standpoint for what they are you can react accordingly and not unwittingly 'feed' the troublesome circumstances.

Opposition leader

Much of what has been said in the preceding pages – about serving all members, political realities and injudicious personal relationships – applies equally to the (or an) opposition leader as to the leader of the council. Nevertheless the whole tenor of the chief executive's dealings with an opposition leader, or inner opposition caucus, is very different. This will have particular impact around that part of the chief executive's role which involves being principal policy adviser.

On policy advice to the opposition, the chief executive is likely ordinarily to be a responder, not an initiator. With the controlling group, you may expect and intend to take a lead yourself, not only responding to and developing or advising on the political objectives and party manifesto commitments of the controlling group, but also yourself spontaneously advising, proposing and leading as you think necessary, or as the relationship between you and them allows. With an opposition party (the largest of them or otherwise), this aspect does not arise, except perhaps by a special council requirement or majority party need or expectation of some kind where all-round briefings and discussions are required or advantageous for some reason. If you are asked to brief the opposition leader about a particular matter or policy proposal, the expectation is that you will indeed do so – it is part of your job. It will, however, largely be on a responsive or reactive, not pro-active, basis.

It is entirely proper, for example, to accede to an opposition request to draft a particular notice of motion or to advise on the potential validity of a proposed procedural approach. It is not proper, however, spontaneously to suggest, or to think up on request, procedural ways of thwarting or embarrassing the controlling group or other administration. That is the role of the opposition if such indeed is the intention. There is a fine line here sometimes, but you must decide where it is and be certain not to cross it. We deal generally with requests for information and research, etc. from opposition members on page 56 below.

Other party leaders

There is usually, in practice, little to differentiate the position of other opposition party leaders from that of the largest opposition party. Two qualifications to this, however, must be noted.

One is that local custom and practice may in fact dictate that the principal opposition leader is acknowledged or recognised – for example, for official consultations, copying of documents or civic invitations – in a way or to a degree which does not apply to the leader of any other opposition party. The second, tending rather in the opposite direction, may arise in a hung or 'balanced' council situation where all or most of the political parties represented on the council have similar numbers of members, and as such have developed different mechanisms accordingly for their mutual dealings.

The latter situation, to which we refer also on pages 56–7, may be extremely taxing for you. Whatever the case, you must ensure that any local customs or practices about such additional opposition groups are acceptable in terms of law and the political proportionality rules, and do not compromise your duties to that group and its constituent members.

If the largest party is only one or two votes short of an overall majority, it may be possible to speak of, and work with, the administration almost as though an overall majority actually existed. But if the situation involves, say, three parties all of about the same size or two roughly equal parties balanced by a third party with few but critical seats, the problems which arise may be acute. It will probably take a lot longer to get anything discussed and decided, formally and informally, and if there is a reluctance to take chairs or risk any form of lead, a virtual deadlock can quickly arise.

It may be possible for you to encourage results in such cases by using your office as neutral ground, venturing advice or initiating leads which cannot come readily from any of the party groups because they are promptly rejected by the others. The delicacy of such situations needs no underlining. In such cases you are likely to benefit particularly from the opportunity to talk through the political, procedural and practical problems with colleagues elsewhere who have experience of the kind of situation you are facing.

Controlling group

If political realities mean that some councillors are more equal than others, that is true too within the controlling (and probably also any other) group. Some in the group will have particular committee or party responsibilities and all are likely to feel some special degree of authority or influence because theirs is the majority party. Yet again, much of what we have already said in relation to the leader of the council applies similarly to those holding the chairs of committees. They too will expect consultations, agenda meetings, a constant stream of intelligence about their subject areas and a substantial degree of political privacy.

To a considerable extent the chief executive can reconcile requirements of this kind quite simply. If the council has appointed various committees and sub-committees, and further appointed particular councillors to become chairs of them and so on, the chief executive is required, as a straightforward matter of instruction to an employee, to accept those decisions and to work to best endeavours accordingly.

It must be remembered, however, that (with exceptions so limited we can disregard them here) a single councillor cannot lawfully be empowered to take any executive decision purporting to bind the council (Local Government Act 1972, section 101(1)). This is no mere fiction. Whatever the influences, a decision taken by a single authorised officer (which *is* lawful) after consultation with a particular councillor – a common formula – is still the decision of the officer, who is answerable and accountable for it. Being a member of the controlling group of itself confers no special legal status or privileges, whatever else it may do.

Opposition groups

Legal developments of recent years have conferred more and better defined rights of particular value to opposition groups (though not of course enacted for them alone). This is especially the case in relation to rights of committee membership and attendance, and of access to information. Opposition members seeking to use these to the full will no doubt from time to time pose dilemmas for you as chief executive and for your senior colleagues.

Despite the fact that everyone recognises opposition groups as inherently different from controlling groups, there is little formally to be said about them. Even the July 1993 report on internal management, referred to earlier on page 50, has nothing extra to say beyond its brief statement in para 5.40. This serves to underline just how important local rules and practices, and your own perception and handling as chief executive of the political interplay between different political groups, are going to be. To tread the path of having to upset each a little in turn will not be easy even if you do comfort yourself with the thought that it's supposed to be a sign that you must be getting the balance about right.

Independents

Although less numerous in local government generally than once they were, independent members are very much still part of the system and still represent a majority of seats on some councils. For chief executives who work for such authorities, all our talk of party control and the relative certainties provided by group decisions has a very different message.

The political groups rules of the Local Government and Housing Act 1989 do not distinguish or exempt independent members in any way. Whether or not in fact they co-ordinate their activities to any extent, independents will be allocated the proportionate balance attributable to their number on the council as a whole.

If the total of independents is indeed a group of individuals and there are no stable alliances amongst them, the effect for the chief executive can be almost as though each of them were a separate political party. They will each be entitled to information, briefing and (perhaps most importantly) *time* as though they were an appointed leader in their own right, which in one sense they are.

Despite the drift of recent legislation, the amount of specific statutory provision about political appointments, relationships and disputes is still quite small. Most chief executives are glad of that. It underlines what, in nearly every case from our experience, is the way chief executives feel about this, probably the most crucial aspect of their work and their personal performance: that every group in every authority and every chief executive are different and that the successful chief executive must forge his or her own set of relationships and find his or her own way. Discussions within SOLACE following publication of the Widdicombe Report in 1986 (*The Conduct of Local Authority Business*, HMSO Cmnd. 9797) showed clearly that the Society as a whole did not favour overregulation of these matters, did not want statutory or artificial protection and placed high on the list the need for every successful chief executive to be seen to rely on nothing but their own capabilities to survive in post.

Just one example of a set of *Guidelines for Member–Employee Relations* is printed as Appendix 3 to this book. What was acceptable in Northampton in 1993 will probably not be exactly, or even nearly, right for anyone else. But with the caveats mentioned on page 96, it may help as a starting point to help you shape your own approach.

The chief officers

Back on pages 18–19 we touched on one aspect of the chief officer relationship: that of the chief executive appointee who previously was one of them and must make the adjustment (as must the others) to the new situation. Working successfully with one's fellow chief officers, and getting the best out of them, cannot rank far behind successful and purposeful political relationships for any new appointee.

We can no more prescribe formulas or norms or ideals here than we can in any other part of this chapter. However, there are some points to think about in what ought to be a conscious and deliberate approach. These points are expectations and performance; equality of treatment; taking time to listen; can they be friends?; and about the team.

Expectations and performance

Some authorities have a formal performance review process for their chief officers, though not all do. The existence of such a mechanism and how it's been used is something else to find out about very early on. Any history of this kind is bound to influence the attitudes and approach of your new colleague chief officers as you meet and begin to settle in with them. As it is often understood that the content of performance review discussions and interviews is not formally recorded, it may be quite difficult to establish what has taken place.

Regardless of that, and even if it is important to be aware of others' perceptions, you must make up your own mind. You must also convey clearly and unambiguously to your chief officers whatever expectations you have of them, particularly if that involves changing well-understood past practice preferred or accepted, for example, by your predecessor. Similarly you must convey what you understand about the expectations of the members concerning them.

One newly appointed chief executive described the 'no surprises' rule he had established for his chief officer colleagues. This referred to his being prepared (within reason) to back them, support their judgements, and help defend whatever it was if the flak began to fly, so long as they had kept him informed where necessary, warned him if some issue or error was about to raise the temperatures, and generally kept him on side. He would not take kindly to being put on the defensive over problems he knew nothing about but evidently should have done.

Weigh up carefully the 'must start as I mean to go on' aspects of your thinking, alongside the 'avoid first impressions/too soon to make judgements' aspects. It's quite logical to make different assessments of different issues. For example, you might reasonably make clear your 'no surprises' rule right from the outset, yet wait weeks or even months before deciding how frequently an officer whose competence you have come to respect needs to keep you up to date about particular matters. This is one of the aspects of getting under the skin of the chief executive job which will inevitably differ greatly according to whether you have been internally appointed or not (see Chapter 2, pages 17–19 in particular), because if you are already familiar with your management team colleagues your own impressions of them are already formed (though they are still forming a significant first impression about *you* and whether you will still behave as the person they recognise or change as you adapt to your new post).

Whether you are an internal or an external appointment, if you identify the kind of problem situation mentioned earlier on page 53 in this chapter, you will have to decide right away how you plan to proceed because your standing or authority may otherwise come into question. The external appointee may well start from a stronger tactical position but any such advantage can be quickly ended and lost by what is perceived as acceptance of, or acquiescence in, whatever situation you inherit.

Equality of treatment

We have rather taken it for granted perhaps, in starting to talk about your fellow chief officers, that you are together organised in some form of formal chief officers' group or management team, since research shows this to be true of virtually every authority. (We discuss a few points about the management team itself on page 102 in Chapter 7.) It is not necessarily true, however, that – disregarding personal incremental points – all your chief officers are paid equally according to the same scale.

Whether the position you inherit is right or not in this respect is something you will soon form an opinion about. This section is concerned with a different aspect of equality, and the fact that your own conduct and style *vis-à-vis* fellow chief officers is probably sending out even more powerful signals around the authority than a salary pecking order (which it will be known you didn't fix anyway). Even if your fellow chief officers are as few as three or four in number, the realities of everyday life mean that inevitably you will see more of some than others, will get on better with some than others, and that work preoccupations and priorities mean you will have more to do with some than others. This is to be expected. It is also likely to be understood as normal by observers of the office politics around you.

Quite differently perceived, though, will be an obvious imbalance in the way you treat your colleagues apart from given external circumstances. If with one or more you are quicker to praise, slower to criticise, better at involving and informing them, are more (or less) confidential, less readily available, or more willing to spend time on whatever issue it is: in each of these cases you are signalling inequality of treatment and accordingly delivering a message, to the disadvantaged in particular, which is bound to undermine their feelings of corporate commitment or belonging fully and equivalently to a team.

In suggesting this we are not saying never talk of one colleague to another or be seen to pass any judgements, but apply the same sort of rules you apply elsewhere to distinguish between normal conversation and mere gossiping or duplicity. Try to behave similarly in similar circumstances, especially when some thing or some factor which ought to be irrelevant but somehow isn't (for example you or the chief officer in question are not of the same sex as the rest of the chief officers or you happen to have known each other a particularly long time) keeps intruding into what you really think you ought to do.

It's important to be fair and impartial in principle between your colleagues. After all, if you cannot demonstrate something about your equal opportunity attitudes amongst your own most senior colleagues, what sort of message will that convey to the rest of your organisation?

Taking time to listen

You will see a good deal of your chief officer colleagues at formal meetings, functions and office discussions. If they work in the same building, use the same lift and park in the same car park, your paths will frequently cross incidentally as well. Probably this means that you will mutually pass on comments, stories, anecdotes and the like which you would not take the trouble deliberately to write or ring up about. This will probably build up a feeling of getting to know each other better and of being readily in touch.

In spite of that, the regular daily to-and-fro may convey a misleading impression that you are also conveying things you want or ought to say to each other. In the busy daily round is there time to listen properly, to let hesitant or submerged thoughts come out and your everyday immediate (and perhaps superficial) impressions to evolve?

> C.Ex developed the practice in discussion with management team members of setting aside about two hours twice a year for each of them to meet on an unstructured basis. It meant C.Ex averaged one such conversation or discussion roughly every month. After any immediate matters of moment, both parties raised wider issues of personal progress or outlook and let conversation develop freely, wherever it would go, for as long as they felt was needed. C.Ex made a considered private effort to hear colleagues' considered or collected thoughts and personal feelings – often very different from the hackneyed exchanges of day-to-day meetings and departmental business.

The issue here is how you build and maintain the right kind of personal contacts and ensure that you are listening as well as hearing, receiving as well as telling, and giving your time to them as well as expecting them to give their time to you.

Can they be friends?

It is obviously important, in the ordinary use of the phrase, to 'get on well' with your chief officer colleagues. Apart from general affability, that may well manifest itself in other ways like office cricket matches, joint invitations to parties or other social events and the like.

You must reflect, however, on the extent to which as head of the paid service and chief executive, your position inevitably sets you apart from your colleagues. You will have to judge their performance, investigate and perhaps report on their failings, and as a matter of routine make decisions about their requests. Can you do, and be seen to do, this even-handedly and correctly if you have developed well-known friendships at a personal level?

We think not. At best, we think you are making it potentially more difficult for yourself. As presumably you will not be friendly similarly with all your colleagues, it breaks the ground rule we suggest above on pages 58–9 about equality of treatment. It also probably displays you to your councillors as potentially compromised or embarrassed should some scandal or problem blow up affecting the chief officer or chief officer's department concerned.

Certainly don't be unfriendly, overformal or stand-offish. But as with leading members (though for other purposes the comparison isn't a good one), keep a little distance between you. That may be all the harder to do if you are an internal appointment who knew people beforehand on a different basis. The time will almost certainly come, however, when you will be glad you did keep that sense of separation. As we said earlier on page 53, friendliness is one thing, friendship another.

The team

The four previous points can be brought together when looking at the relationship between the chief executive and the management team. One of the key skills for any chief executive is the ability to create synergy within the team, to foster the developments of roles within the team and above all to build the team into an effective group. 'Our team' is more effective than 'my team'.

Employees generally

As important as your key political and chief officer relationships undoubtedly are, it would be wrong to imply that your fellow employees at large aren't also significant. You will probably regard your own general rapport with your colleagues at every level as yet another critical factor for success, and indeed many chief executives now make a point of emphasising the broad varying nature of their relationships across the whole spectrum of employees. At every opportunity they signal that *everyone* in their organisation counts, whatever job they do. The tendency to refer to the highest and lowest in establishments is a product of the hierarchical structure which has traditionally created all those levels. As flatter structures emerge, the difference lessens – and in this era of competition, efficiency and budgetary restraint, surely everyone in your organisation is now there by deliberate intent because you want them filling that particular niche and not because there was a vacancy in an establishment.

As chief executive, the managerial leader, you have a number of symbols of office, many of which are also synonymous with power in the organisation. Your office itself and its furnishings, your support staff, your car, your seating position in meetings, etc. all demonstrate *rank*. But they came with the job, probably; you were given them. And if you can be *given* managerial rank, you have to *learn* managerial competence and you have to *earn* employee respect. Refer to what on page 45 we call 'big boots syndrome', try to appreciate more how others see you and acknowledge that the privilege and advantages of being head of the paid service can have their downside in terms of inhibiting everyday relationships with fellow employees generally.

It is trite to say that acknowledging people is important but you cannot give them their worth unless you recognise them for what they are, as experienced, as individualists, as team players, etc. Staying in touch and keeping your finger on the pulse is a perpetual and difficult process. It will be important for you to make a conscious assessment of the variety of employee relationships, according to the size of your authority, and work out what you can achieve and what you can *sustain* in terms of your relationships with all the other employees.

The trade unions, the press and other key relationships

Look back at pages 32–3 in Chapter 2, where we listed the people and agencies identified by a group of new chief executives as important, or relevant in regard to developing contacts and links. The whole list will not be relevant for everyone. But if even half the headings are on your personal list, they amount to a substantial commitment.

They also differ in character from the types of relationship covered in the earlier part of this chapter. What we have been talking about here have been internal to the authority and crucial for the most basic aspects of your work as a chief executive. The list on pages 32–3 is about external relationships almost exclusively and while you may not want to suggest, even privately to yourself, that they are unimportant, they are secondary to your central member and officer frameworks and will not all rank the same in your estimate of priorities.

There will nevertheless be a reason why you identify each of the names or bodies on your own list as significant for your work as chief executive. Obviously enough that presupposes that a good working relationship can significantly help you. It is not overelaboration of this theme to suggest that it is worth spending a few moments thinking through in each case why you identified each link, what you want out of that link and your relationship with them in each case, and what they may in turn want or expect out of you.

Let us first take the trade unions in particular, represented as they are probably partly within and partly external to the authority. When a dispute or other problem arises, you will want to be able to discuss matters on a sound personal basis, if you can, with those whose job it is to represent the grouping involved. This is much less likely if you have not previously established some kind of rapport or relationship which both sides can call upon when they have a job to do in an atmosphere which may make formal exchanges and negotiations difficult.

> C.Ex had a quarterly off-the-record discussion with trade union representatives at which there was no specific agenda. He found this a valuable two-way opportunity, both to hear general concerns from the trade unions and also to outline his own thoughts on the 'big issues' facing the organisation.

It sometimes happens that in a national dispute, authorities do not want to add the force of local grievance to whatever issues form the base of the principal cause of action. This inevitably means finely judged handling of the local situation, and you are likely to have good cause to be thankful for the time and effort you have put into a relationship that allows a degree of mutual understanding which may not be obtainable through formal channels.

Parallel circumstances are likely to arise, which you can well imagine for yourself, in relation to your identified key links and outside organisations. Another obvious grouping for most will be the press or media. Relationships there perhaps share a number of characteristics with the trade unions: a set of different ends to serve, and a potential for wide variation between attitudes or actions which you (or your authority) regard as helpful, restrained or responsible on the one hand, and questioning, distracting, provocative or even mischievous on the other. Sometimes they can exhibit both at once in different contexts.

Even if you have a skilled and respected press or public relations officer, you will often be quoted by the press and they will often want to speak to you personally. If you want their discretion on item A, you may expect to have to earn it by frankness on item B. Ground rules about what is and is not 'on the record' have to be explicitly understood – but if you really want to avoid the wrong quote appearing, better not to say it in the first place! Always remember that positive media coverage makes a major contribution to the image of local government and can enhance respect for local democracy.

Everyone has a variety of other relationships of particular significance to them at any given time. It may be, for example, that one particular person links, or leads for you, on an area of work of special importance such as a major capital project or a local development corporation with whose activities you must keep regularly in touch.

It may be a particular politician – the chairman or (lord) mayor of the authority – or, indeed, a councillor with whom you have additional dealings for whatever reason, even though he/she is not one of the formal leadership/chairs/spokesperson groupings. It may alternatively be someone outside the authority but important for your role within it, like a mentor or action learning set colleague (see pages 81–3), or an external auditor. You can easily construct your own long list.

Each relationship on that list will be different. The mix of personalities is different; some you have formal authority over, some have it over you. In some cases, as perhaps with a civic head, you may at the same time be combining guidance with deference. In working at the right kind of relationship for any situation, we are back again to attributes like tact, diplomacy and judgement – all readily recognised 'soft' chief executive skills.

What we are saying in this chapter about relationships, and how you may use them to get the best out of people, is hardly new. Nearly 2500 years ago Xenophon described how Cyrus set about it. This appears in a passage which the Loeb Classical Library translates as follows:

In the first place, then, he showed at all times as great kindness of heart as he could; for he believed that just as it is not easy to love those who seem to hate us, or to cherish goodwill toward those who bear us ill-will, in the same way those who are known to love and to cherish good-will could not be hated by those who believe themselves loved. (*Cyropaedia*, VIII, ii, 1)

Earlier, at V, iii, 47–51, Cyrus anticipates much of the managing through people and management by walking around philosophies of modern times by the following:

Hereupon [his commanders] went to their tents, and as they went, they remarked to one another what a good memory Cyrus had and how he called every one by name as he assigned them their places and gave them their instructions. Now Cyrus made a study of this; for he thought it passing strange that, while every mechanic knows the names of the tools of his trade and the physician knows the names of all the instruments and medicines he uses, the general should be so foolish as not to know the names of the officers under him and yet he must employ them as his instruments not only whenever he wishes to capture a place or defend one, but also whenever he wishes to inspire courage or fear. And whenever Cyrus wished to honour anyone, it seemed to him proper to address him by name. Furthermore it seemed to him that those who were conscious of being personally known to their general exerted themselves more to be seen doing something good and were more ready to abstain from doing anything bad. And when he wanted a thing done, he thought it foolish to give orders as do some masters in their homes: 'Some one go get water!' 'Some one split wood!' for when orders are given in that way, all, he thought, looked at one another and no one carried out the order; all were to blame, but no one felt shame or fear as he should, because he shared the blame with many. It was for this reason, therefore, that he himself spoke to every one by name to whom he had any command to give. Such at least, was Cyrus's opinion about this matter.

We would not choose such language today, perhaps, but human nature still defines relationships as two-way processes. The clichés which attach to the need to work consciously at them only serve to emphasise, rather than diminish, their importance.

Chapter 5

Some processes that count

- Mapping the ground
- The budget process
- Handling negotiations
- Employee development
- Managing the members

Mapping the ground

Chapter 9 of Janice Morphet's book *The Role of Chief Executives in Local Government* (Longman, 1993) tries to answer the question (to which we referred in Chapter 1 at pages 5–6) what do chief executives do? It does so in role descriptive terms, as did the Audit Commission's 1989 study *More Equal than Others* (they may have meant *less* equal!). One 1989 study survey quoted (p. 169) gave the highest percentage score (at 26 per cent twice the score given to 'political manager') to the descriptive label 'corporate manager' in terms of what the sampled chief executives recorded as their most preferred roles and activities. Similarly, Chapter 9 of Alan Norton's 1991 INLOGOV study on *The Role of Chief Executive in British Local Government* seeks to define the tasks of the chief executive, primarily in terms of the 54 main tasks identified by questionnaire respondents. In the same year, Michael Clarke and Professor John Stewart in the short SOLACE/LGMB paper on *The Role of the Chief Executive* opined that 'the role is more readily understood by its organisational position than by the activities for which the chief executive is responsible', and that the 'role is determined by relationships rather than by a set of activities' (p. 1). Between those two quotations, Clarke and Stewart pinpoint four aspects to the role which evidently define for them the cornerstones of the job: being at the key interface between the staff and the organisation and the politicians, being principal policy adviser, being head of the council's paid service and being an ambassador for the whole authority.

This chapter does not set out to rework the carefully researched studies of writers such as these. Rather we wish to spend a few pages underpinning what for us are a few practical realities which may easily get lost in the philosophising and theorising about the role. We refer to four key aspects or activities in particular: the budget process, the handling of negotiations, employee development, and finally – and at somewhat greater length – what we have loosely called 'managing the members'.

The budget process

In his 1986 book *Job at the Top: The chief executive in local government*, Sir John Boynton (clerk and chief executive of Cheshire County Council in the 1960s and 1970s) devotes one of his earlier chapters specifically to the process of the budget and finance (pp. 42–53).

Sir John begins by saying: 'Of all the decisions taken by a local authority none is more important than the budget. It both sets future policy and reflects past policy decisions. It goes without saying that the chief executive should be fully involved in every aspect of budget formulation.' Whatever else may have changed in the years since the days when Sir John managed Cheshire with such distinction, his point about the importance of the budget process has not. It has become even more important in the world of government constraints, declining resources and SSAs in which we now work.

Most chief executives wouldn't consider it vital to try to know how every line in the budget book was made up; what is important is to understand the structure of the budget, where any 'hidden reserves' are held or particular flexibility is available, and how reliable are your budget monitoring processes, so that you can thereby master the strategy of this year's budget and therefore lead and influence the production of next year's.

In the world of grant-related expenditure assessments (GREAs) and targets in the early 1980s, the city treasurer had provided an accurate but lengthy and complex analysis of the rather unusual position derived for the authority. C.Ex largely discarded it, and provided a 2- or 3-page plain English guide to the total spend available and the bids from the respective committees' draft estimates. It was important that every member had some idea of the new system and the cash considerations involved, written in short, everyday terms they were more likely to read. At the same time it served to illustrate the role of the chief executive in leading discussion of a process with which his predecessor had been known to have seemingly little concern.

Handling negotiations

The handling of negotiations is a much underrated skill or competency for chief executives, success in which has always had the power to make or break a reputation. Around the outbreak of war in 1939 the brilliant but flawed town clerk, Leslie Heeler, who had already upset his members early in his appointment, was reportedly saved by the admitted expert handling of his case over the threatened future of the town's municipal airport (and it was another two decades before he was finally dismissed).

C.Ex was offered the job at the end of the interviews, but at less than the point of scale he considered would justify the move. Accordingly he accepted conditionally on a higher point, and when questioned about it said simply: 'Why should you think I would represent the *authority* properly in negotiations if I couldn't speak up on behalf of myself?' The authority paid up.

Paragraph 33 of the JNC conditions of service for chief executives reads that: 'No major negotiations relating to the functions or duties of the council shall be initiated or carried on by any other officer of the council except with the cognisance of the chief executive.' This little-quoted provision indicates the importance of this aspect of the chief executive's role, which was officially attached to it from the outset in the early 1970s.

Good judgement, however, is required to decide how and when you should personally involve yourself in any particular negotiations. 'Cognisance' in paragraph 33 simply means prior knowledge and acquiescence, and not necessarily personal intervention, and it is hardly prudent to try to lead negotiations on a topic on which you are not adequately briefed about the background, or the scope or latitude within which satisfactory outcomes may be derived. As with the handling of complaints, there will be times when it is canny not to become directly and personally involved too soon because, for example:

1. It might undermine the position of your employees who have dealt with the issue so far, who will have to deal with like issues again in the future, and who do not need a signal which may be read as your lacking in confidence in them.
2. You may have to become formally involved later and so need to preserve for a while longer your independent position above partiality on the disputes involved.
3. You may inadvertently short-circuit the intended processes for the future and thereby encourage people always to refer things like this to you straight away, which you (and no doubt others) can do without.
4. The people dealing with the problem now may resolve it anyway, and/or actually do it better than you would have done.

Employee development

If *you* are persuaded that you need to pay attention to your own personal development during your tenure as chief executive, arguably a considerable proportion of your employees are likely to think *their* needs are even greater.

They may well perceive you as having 'made it', whereas they have to continue thinking about their futures in a climate where longer-term planning is increasingly uncertain. More difficult still, qualifications are less achievements for life than once they were, with more and more bodies requiring continuing professional development (see also page 12).

This is not the place to try to discuss the wide-ranging theme of employee development and the many ways you might pursue it. We simply make the point that it is, in our opinion, an area of vital concern with a significant part to play in the way you are judged overall.

'Managing the members'

The tag phrase we have chosen carries no more connotation of manipulation than other suggestions that you have to work deliberately at a particular relationship to put your best into it and so get the best out of it.

Both of us over the past decade and more have become aware of many cases (a hundred or more over that period) in which relationships between chief executives and their leading members or councils have broken down. In a significant number of cases (by no means all) it seems clear that the problems have occurred as a result of (or been considerably contributed to by) the conduct, attitude, style or approach of the chief executive.

From these observations we offer the following 10 points as do's and don'ts. In themselves they neither guarantee success nor early retirement, but in the shifting world of local politics and alliances we are talking 'brownie points and percentages', about factors which can make that vital difference. Again, we set them out in no particular order.

Assess the political realities

Make a conscious effort to assess the pattern of power and influence in and around the authority and its political groups. Assessing and reacting accordingly is not the same as interfering, but you cannot be politically adroit (small *and* large p), if you are insensitive to who matters more, whose star is rising or falling, and what are the issues which, small or large to an outsider, are vital priorities within the groups – or alternatively are programmes and priorities which will be sacrificed to expediency if need arises, rather than being maintained at all costs.

As circumstances alter cases, so 'the political realities' at any given time are likely to be always subtly shifting and evolving. Here again, you have to use your judgement to decide when to be different from precedent or example elsewhere. As SOLACE president John Horsnell (Isle of Wight) put it to a group of newly appointed chief executives in January 1994, discussing advice from a colleague chief executive to follow a lead: 'My reality may simply not let me do what (s)he is doing.' You must, in short, catch the mood of your authority and everything happening inside it. If, for example, on election day you wear a tie or other clothing of a colour predominantly associated in that day's context with one of the political parties involved, don't be surprised if some people think you're sending a signal.

Cultivate the members

Inevitably there is a divide between members and employees. Individually they supposedly have no powers legally to commit the council, which is distinct from the sum of however many parts there are. In practical reality, however, the council's perception of you is a consensus or collection of separate opinions based on differing private experiences.

It is foolish not to be pragmatic about this, and despite the political realities about control, chairing committees, etc. (decided in any event by the council, not by you), foolish also not to give any meaning to being the servant of the whole council. Avoid servility or being obsequious, which no one admires, but be accessible and even-handed with what we have often called in this book 'the political realities'. If you promise a copy letter or whatever, take a few seconds to send it quickly; telephone back if asked; refuse politely, cheerfully and with justification if you have to; and so on.

In short, try to give members positive experiences of dealing with you, and no avoidable private reasons for joining action to your detriment should they get the chance. It's a tendency in many of us to put up with a lot but, given something more serious or a pejorative judgement by others, to quote or make an issue of something which ordinarily we would have let pass. 'And I'll tell you another thing so-and-so did . . .': it's the classic kick-them-when-they're-down syndrome.

Never give members a choice between party loyalty and you

Almost certainly you'll lose, and if temporarily you don't appear to have lost, you may very well be seen to have done so in the long run. Party or group loyalties are understandably very important to members and the party favour ultimately provides the ticket to council membership (or at least candidature). It is unrealistic to expect members, however well you think you have come to know them or work with them in the past, to jeopardise their own status and position on behalf of yours. And if 'members' in this context really means the leader or a leading group member, they have to watch and safeguard their own position too. Being too closely identified with you, or a losing political faction or line, is bad news for them as well.

C.Ex worked primarily to a meeting of five 'group officers' who got together every four weeks or so to go through prospective issues and draft reports, and to consider progress on the 63 specific commitments in the election manifesto on which the group had won its seats. Over two or three years the five had become so used to the presence of C.Ex at these meetings that they openly discussed between them their own party political concerns. C.Ex found it salutary, having wondered what he could 'get through the group' himself (starting with them), then to hear the five discussing what they could themselves get through the full party group meeting later.

Be seen to take the lead

Many chief executives feel that their job is much more about the exercise of influence than the exercise of overt power. Be that as it may, any chief executive who is not perceived as being out at the front of the organisation is sooner or later bound to be in difficulties, because he or she will demonstrably (in the opinion of others) not be performing the twin roles of principal policy adviser and head of the paid service.

Taking the lead need not always mean being first, loudest or longest over an issue. It may involve a good deal of activity which is not, and is not meant to be, visible to others (for example, advice or information to leading members ahead of committee reports and decisions). Nevertheless the extent to which you make or initiate events, or to which they always seem to come to you first, will be clear to those around you. Likewise they will perceive your personal priorities with greater clarity than you expect: indeed, from the point of view of public opinion within the authority, probably with greater clarity than you do. It is only pragmatic to realise these things and act accordingly, especially when you are newly appointed, still rapidly making impressions, and frankly in need of 'a few wins' to start off with.

Involve yourself in civic and community life

Though the civic profile of authorities varies greatly, and so does the nature and make-up of the authority's area which you serve, you cannot pretend that the role of a chief executive is confined to working inside the organisation with no profile outside it.

Professor Janice Morphet found that 'chief executives do not like being dignitaries', though she goes on to add that 'it is not clear whether this is a dislike of trailing round behind a mayor or leader, or whether this essentially figure head role is really perceived by chief executives as a waste of time' (*The Role of Chief Executives in Local Government*, Longman, 1993, p. 172).

An obvious moral in such cases is not to apply for a job which clearly involves a high civic profile (with the hours and partner participation which probably go with it). Yet we think it is superficial simply to write off civic events as a waste of the chief executive's personal time.

There is, of course, a balance to be struck between such events and other duties but they are likely to comprise part of the job description and must be given their due as such. Those who have not been close to the civic role in earlier jobs (and may think it somehow compromises their dignity as a real manager) often find later that they have underestimated the community importance and significance of this aspect of the job. It is important to be consistent in this respect and not to support community spirit and social cohesion in, say, housing capital programmes on the one hand, while ignoring its traditional manifestations in other contexts.

This heading is not confined to civic events in the literal mayoral or chairmanship sense. You will receive a lot of invitations to, and have a lot of opportunities to take part in, other events and activities in your area. Bearing in mind the point we made on page 25 about setting an example you can sustain, accepting a well-chosen proportion of what comes along will give you the chance to meet a different (and perhaps influential) cross-section of people in your area, give you valuable feedback on how others perceive the authority and its performance, and also give you the chance to make valuable contacts and exercise influence to the advantage of your authority and your role in trying to lead its policy advice and management structures.

Whether they like it or not, effective chief executives learn to perform well as civic dignitaries when required. Janice Morphet's commentary on this role quoted above goes on to say:

> There is an interesting comparison here with the private sector, where many chief executives have considerable difficulty in managing public events such as annual general meetings when they frequently have to be rehearsed. Perhaps chief executives prefer an active management role rather than a more public one.

Stay formal with members

For many the respectful, formal style of address employed in council meetings and other public occasions is now old-fashioned and unnatural. Certainly those used to local government in places like the USA, Australia and New Zealand often find the British way of municipal life much more formal than they are accustomed to. All this is largely a matter of taste, local custom and, perhaps, the age (or age relationship) of the people concerned.

We are not advocating that you should be stuffy or pompous, or always say 'sir' here and 'madam chairman' (or whatever is preferred) there. Most people are more comfortable using, and receiving, a relaxed and straightforward manner than anything which seems at all artificial or forced. And what you would say across a public meeting is likely to be regarded on both sides as necessarily different from what would be appropriate in a private conversation taking place, say, away from the authority at a conference.

The key distinction for us is between overformality and overfamiliarity. The latter may be seen as trespassing on the space of reserve that should exist between you and the members. *They* can be very informal and familiar with *you*; it is not necessary to reciprocate fully. If you do, it may cause you embarrassment later, and even serious compromise, if duty requires you to take some formal steps affecting that member, or an attempt is made to abuse a special line to your door which that member feels he or she has. Furthermore, others will be observant of your familiarity which may be seen to undermine your otherwise even-handed treatment of members.

It goes without saying that what crosses the line into unwise familiarity or closeness of relationship will differ widely. Someone may be a personal friend of long standing from well before the member–officer relationship arose. People know this but they will expect you to have the judgement to handle it wisely. In any event, that good a friend will hardly need telling for, from their political standpoint, they won't want to be compromised either. Bearing in mind what we said above (see page 69) about the power of political loyalties, remember how easily a personal situation may be turned against you, or perceived to your detriment, if apparently 'safe' circumstances change. A good guide is to ask yourself whether you would be having this particular conversation or encounter if you weren't chief executive. If the answer is 'no', it is a signal that you are in at least some respects on duty and your behaviour and demeanour should be appropriate to that fact.

Keep accessible to employees and unions

The largest authorities may have as many as two hundred or more times the number of employees of smaller authorities, and clearly the chief executive who can readily find time soon to meet an individual employee out of 200 or so could hardly offer the same facility to 50,000.

But everybody else realises that too. The important factor is that people should have the perception that you are approachable, visible and 'around' rather than unrecognised and remote. That doesn't mean they expect necessarily to have any one-to-one time with you, but if they feel they could do if they really needed to, you've done well. (Sometimes their standards of what's worthy of your personal time seem higher than yours anyway.)

It's important, especially at the start of your time as chief executive when you are establishing your style and approach, to make time for what we may call accessibility (and that's more than 'walking the job' which all the management texts talk about). The situation of your office itself will play a part in this. One of us has a door off a corridor that normally stands open so that anyone outside can judge for themselves whether to go in or interrupt. If the door is shut it's perceived that probably it's not the right moment: a meeting is going on or something else which requires some more private time (it may only be long enough to eat a sandwich at lunchtime!).

Whatever you do, think consciously about whether your lifestyle in the authority encourages perceptions of relevance or remoteness, access or absence. And make time for contacts which common sense tells you will be particularly important to your reputation or where you may on occasion need some understanding and co-operation. Contacts like that perhaps most obviously include the trade unions but you will be able to make your assessment for your own authority.

Use professional principles as a last resort

It seems that, for some bees at least, they possess a powerful sting but die if they use it. Presumably bees know that, but it is remarkable how frequently people perceive themselves as possessed of defence mechanisms or supposed strengths which others assess as largely illusory. There is an anecdote of a US president describing how he found in a sudden crisis that there was enough nuclear fire power available to him in the problem locality to liquidate half the hemisphere, but no properly equipped commandos or assault troops who would have been far more useful in practical terms.

The moral of that anecdote for chief executives is that you are far more likely to win arguments or gain influence by a sound professional approach of merit, coupled with a judicious blend of tactics, pragmatism and common sense, than you will be trying to quote and rely on your supposed seniority.

> C.Ex was confronted by his deputy, who felt that his status as deputy was not rightfully accorded by the seating plan for some civic occasion. 'Don't they know who I am?' he asked the C.Ex, who at once replied: 'Why, who *are* you, X?'

It may be quite appropriate and even necessary on some occasions to refer to your position as head of the paid service, or paragraph 33 of your conditions of service about the conduct of negotiations (see page 67 above), or your duty as monitoring officer or chief financial officer if you are one. Nevertheless, these roles are best worn lightly. Once you are quoting formalities by the book you are risking great compromise to your position if you lose.

You want your authority to be voluntarily accepted for what it is, rather than just legalistically for who you are. Compromise the lesser issues without feeling you have sold short your professional standing as a chief executive, because we all do it. Reserve the standing on rights and ceremonies for when you really need to use them and when others can see you have to do so even if they don't agree with you on the merits of the case involved.

In most authorities it's difficult to gauge just how much authority the members have really given the chief executive. It's even harder to judge when to use that authority on a formal basis.

Appearances matter less than actualities

You can undoubtedly do a great deal to strengthen or weaken perceptions of you (and perhaps, too, your own level of self-esteem) by your personal style. In an age when individuality is applauded in theory but often mistrusted in practice, image is undoubtedly important as a factor in calibrating the success or impact of your dealings with whoever your recipient or target 'audience' are. Like a first impression, a poor image is more damaging and harder to correct long term than a neutral impression is to worsen. Note what we say on page 30 about 93 per cent of first impressions being based on non-verbal assessment and the reason why image is so important (a key factor which lies behind the growing interest in the subject).

Many times already in this book we have given advice which comes down to saying 'behave like a chief executive ought to behave' (even though you should have the courage and self-confidence to be different if there are good reasons for doing so). We are no less ready to counsel you to 'look the part' both physically and metaphorically in whatever mode that applies for you and your circumstances.

But remember, too, that what is superficial will not last long in the wear and tear of life. Those around you will judge whether anything of substance lies behind the packaging, the fashion, the politically-correct-but-perceived-as-token meaningless gesture which is seen to be just a front. Looking and acting the part won't be much good if people think that you can't actually *be* it. Appearances aren't just about clothing and walking the job, they're about the fundamentals of whether your members and employees think you're holding the job down or whether it's holding you down.

Write from the head and not from the heart

A large proportion of all council files are open to public, or at least member, scrutiny these days and that in itself may pose dilemmas in many councils for officers who are endeavouring to provide confidential advice even-handedly to different political groups. Whether or not your letter or whatever is intended for publication as such, it's best to assume that it might be shown where you don't expect it to be and to maintain in it a professional tone accordingly unmixed with inappropriate personal emotions.

That is not to say that everything should be neutral, laconic, anodyne: far from it. It is quite proper and professional to express advice with clear preferences and to choose words of pace and persuasion where occasion demands. But it should always be clear that they are appropriate to your role as chief executive, and not merely gratuitous private preference.

A second principle is not to send off letters too quickly which are influenced by strong feelings of anger or indignation. They are unlikely to be measured and modulated responses if written in the heat of the moment, especially as (unlike some less senior officers) you have the ability to stop the office while you fire off your response without delay (probably these days by fax).

Make a point of not sending off that kind of letter until you've slept on it if it contains phrases you know you wouldn't normally use and might regret later. You may even think of a better phrased succinct response, given time, which will make your point without dragging you into the kind of insult-swopping which probably got you going in the first place.

> C.Ex, who had fifteen years or more in post, was incensed by what he considered unfair criticism of him uttered in a council meeting by a member known to 'blow his top' unpredictably in the face of injustices. He wrote a vigorous defence. Seeing the office carbons the C.Ex's deputy diffidently asked whether the C.Ex thought he would gain anything by sending the letter. At once the C.Ex rang to order the top copy destroyed, and didn't send anything. Nothing more in fact was heard of the member's supposed criticisms.

As we said before, observance of the foregoing points won't guarantee success or effectiveness in themselves. But they may help to keep you out of trouble and, in a difficult corner, make that vital little difference to your leaving much less material for anyone to get hold of you with.

All in all your style of 'managing the members' adds up to the way you approach one of the most crucial aspects of your job, apart from the particular relationships we discuss on pages 48–64 in Chapter 4. Think of all the above points together adding up to your *corporate body language* and work consciously on them accordingly.

Chapter 6

Some ways of helping

- Feedback
- Mentoring
- Action learning
- Networking
- Time management

'Of course I can cope – I'm a chief executive!'

Light-hearted words in 1993 from Barry Harris, chief executive of the Waikato Regional Council in New Zealand, but not spoken, of course, without some truth behind them or without some inherited expectation that goes with the job.

The expectation may come from others or from yourself or very likely from both sources. And at times it may be a considerable burden, as well as a stimulus, to feel that others are presuming or relying on you, and that it really is down to you to provide leadership on some issue or to sort out some mess. We have already discussed the stresses and strains which may arise in pages 43–4 in Chapter 3.

This chapter is concerned with some specific ways of helping to assess your progress and performance, helping you to relate to and learn from the work of others, and to take space and strength from doing so. Together with what we say in Chapter 3, it may well be helpful when particularly stressful or difficult situations have arisen but it is not exclusively for that purpose. Just as routine maintenance may forestall breakdown maintenance, so are benchmarks and indicators helpful in healthy everyday situations as a way of marking out and assessing your own personal development.

Feedback

A famous American mayor of a major city reportedly used to call out 'How am I doing?' to all and sundry as his way of keeping in touch with reality.

You're unlikely to want to copy that particular style but there is a great deal to be said for trying to assess your own performance and (if you can) to glimpse how the organisation sees you. In one sense this is just an aspect of the overall theme of communication, but it has other aspects. For one thing, it may be very difficult to receive (or accept at face value and trust) direct comment about yourself from subordinates.

> C.Ex was doing a presentation to a small but significant audience. There were introductory comments based on some soundings about his reputation within the authority. C.Ex was struck by a reported comment that he had a capacity for knowing what was going on everywhere. It seemed a helpful attribute but as he was inwardly all too conscious of areas where he should ideally know much more, he wondered if his real skill didn't lie in making people think he knew more than he really did. A useful attribute perhaps, but a very different one.

It is extremely difficult for any chief officer, let alone the chief executive, to be sure about their level of knowledge and performance within an organisation. You may be the last to hear an office rumour or find that your secretary tells you things on an unofficial collective behalf that either other people daren't tell you, would prefer not to tell you or tell the secretary on the unspoken but deliberate assumption that it will be passed on to you. One of us, Roger Morris at Northampton, for some years parked in a rather isolated position and commonly ran up flights of stairs to his office. A move to a new building then converted this to use of a much larger parking area and several daily sets of chance meetings with people in the lifts. He was conscious of speaking informally to a far larger number of people, most of whom would never in a formal context have approached him.

Feedback can take many forms, but it may be helpful to categorise six sources which you may want consciously to assess as both different and complementary. These are feedback (i) from leading members, (ii) from members generally, (iii) from other employees, (iv) from colleagues outside the authority, (v) from family or friends and (vi) from other external sources. We will look at each of these in turn.

Feedback from leading members

Since not only your effectiveness and performance, but ultimately your survival in the job, depend to such a large extent on the opinions and continuing consent of leading members, it is important to take conscious note of all the available signals as well as any formal expressions of opinion.

If there is no formal system for performance review in your authority you may very well want to create one, even if initially the system only applies to you personally. Performance review – or an equivalent evaluation or appraisal mechanism – is a fertile source of benefits. Not only can it provide a ready opportunity to deal with and discharge issues at an early stage which might, if left unresolved, become much more serious, but it prevents members reaching so easily any subsequent decision critical of priorities and progress in which they have regularly shared. Not all situations will allow you to reach a position where you can feel that you and the members jointly own key aspects of your work programme and priorities, but that shouldn't prevent you achieving what commonly staked-out ground you can in the circumstances.

Remember that 'leading members' here doesn't just mean politicians of a controlling party. You have to have regard to the political realities of being the servant to the whole council – even if most are independents or there is a balanced situation – and that will always be important even if the council's will is expressed through a political majority.

> C.Ex came into a post with no context of performance review or equivalent. After a year in post he wrote a public report for the policy committee agenda referring to what he'd done and asking for views, advice on priorities or whatever.
>
> The first time members passed his report very quickly without recorded comment (which gave him a useful signal in itself). He did a similar report each year and gradually value developed in the process which came to be properly discussed on the private part of the agenda.

It would of course be a mistake to rely totally on a performance review process. You can find out quite a lot by analysing for yourself a variety of other responses and factors. For example, are members willing to trust you with delegated powers to sort out particular issues which arise? Are they likely to ask you to draft speeches or letters or whatever, and do they use the results extensively? Do they show some reasonableness at distinguishing between your accountability on the one hand and the fact that you can't personally know everything, do everything, and be at personal fault for everything on the other? Overreadiness to find trivial fault, as opposed to being supportive, is clearly an unwelcome sign and an important one (even if the real problems are objectively considered to lie more with them than with you). Much of this adds up to your requiring continuing personal and political sensitivity to what's going on around you and needing to keep your ear to the ground.

Feedback from members generally

Much of the previous section also applies here. Whatever the political majority (or lack of one) in your authority, you cannot forget that you are the employee of the whole council. It is no easy task to give satisfaction to an administration on the one hand that you are effectively leading the implementation of their programme, and on the other satisfy an opposition that you are doing your rather different duty by them as well. And, of course, today's opposition may be tomorrow's administration and today's chair tomorrow's backbencher.

If as chief executive you naturally see a greater proportion of the same few leading members – probably overlapping with the relatively few who carry out formal review of your performance – then it's a good idea to remember that a large part of the whole council see you a lot less, know you less and form their impressions of you from a greater distance than that of regular personal contact. They may feel those things entitle them to claim your attention more readily on the occasions when they want to.

Refer back to what we said in the last chapter on pages 68–75 about aspects of 'managing members': the chief executive who has that happy knack of making everyone particularly welcome or special is bound to have a head start.

One of us, Roger Paine both at Cardiff and in his previous chief executive post, has first-hand experience of spending time with members away from the City Hall in the more informal setting of a 'ward meeting'. These occasions would often take place on site, touring around a ward, meeting people and seeing issues 'on the ground'. In this setting, members often feel more comfortable discussing 'their' agenda. Inevitably discussion widens to the performance of the chief executive himself, of the departments and the top managers. Repeated annually, this kind of process can monitor changes. Each time it was carried out the perception of members, and their willingness to discuss issues, became sharper and more open.

Feedback from other employees

The loneliness of the chief executive position, and the fact that everyone is by definition less senior, combine to make the receipt and evaluation of feedback from employees much more difficult. One newly appointed chief executive was advised by his former chief executive never to ask fellow chief officers how he was doing because he couldn't believe whatever answer he got. This may be true, though some will choose to interpret the answer rather than have no answer at all.

You may well have, particularly on your immediate personal staff, one or two people with whom you can discuss, more or less openly, issues and opinions which you couldn't ventilate elsewhere in the authority. That may be very helpful (even if there are some dangers in you being perceived as having any special alliances, confidences or favouritisms). If you have to be reticent about accepting at face value anything said to you about personal performance issues, be on the look out for what has been left unsaid, for clearly you cannot cut yourself off from any evaluation of the opinions and comments from employees around you.

C.Ex was newly appointed but had held the same post elsewhere already. As part of his introductory process, he included a specific request for the senior colleagues, etc. he was meeting to say what they expected of him. He knew this process would have limitations but worked on the basis that something would be much better than nothing and that he could return to, and explore satisfaction levels with, their announced expectations at periodic stages later.

Feedback from colleagues outside the authority

This is an important source of encouragement which should not be neglected and we say more about it in the section on networking later in this chapter. Colleague chief executives in particular understand your role and the inner processes the job entails. If working for neighbouring authorities, they are likely to know a useful amount about the political and situational background of your authority. They will hear their own members' comments, and their own observations from the everyday local government dealings of one authority with another. As a result they can give you advice, warnings or other feedback unaffected by the kinds of prejudices and protected positions of your own authority. Professional knowledge and your interest at heart represent a powerful combination.

Feedback from family or friends

Your family and friends are positioned quite differently from people in and around your authority. Probably they do not carry the local government baggage around with them but they are in touch with other taxpayers, citizens and customers of the authority and may yield you useful, if anecdotal, evidence about things.

Knowing them as you do, you may find it rather easier to read the information that you get for what it is. A lukewarm or polite feedback on something may be influenced by deference or courtesy to you, but if they go further than strictly necessary for that, and actually sound enthusiastic, it's usually reasonable to assume rather more than the minimum.

Don't neglect the fact, either, that your family and friends see a different you from the official version that goes to work. They probably aren't conscious at all of any chief executive 'aura' or status problems that help to isolate you at work, and they may be quick to spot signs of stress or pressure before you are aware of them yourself. They may also tell you things – about your style of dress or image, for instance – which you won't find out at work.

Feedback from other external sources

In Chapter 2 (pages 32–3) we spoke of all the various external organisations and agencies that are important to your area and to you. They, and many other groups of less obvious or less immediate priority, may provide you with a good deal of information, comment, anecdote, praise or complaint which will be useful intelligence-gathering for you about how you and your authority are perceived in the context in question.

Some of it will come from secondary motives. They may be challenging decisions, enlisting support, seeking a grant or there may be other good reasons why you shouldn't necessarily accept at face value all you hear. But the more listening and interpreting you do, the broader your knowledge base from which to judge what you hear. It's a good idea to allow your natural instincts and gut feelings every chance to develop; you have an advantage which few people if any apart from chief executives have the opportunity to equal.

Mentoring

Having a mentor obviously isn't unique to chief executives or local government but it can be particularly valuable to you as chief executive because of the characteristics (which we particularly discussed in Chapter 3) of the loneliness and isolation of the job.

The ability to talk to someone who has known you a long time and who has a particular interest and stake in your progress and well-being is important in itself but mentoring is more of a two-way activity than that. A true mentor is not just there to be called upon but also encourages, supports, advises and warns of his or her own volition. Many chief executives can look back to a particularly significant early career relationship with someone whose example and practical support has led later to a lasting respect and friendship. Both of us writing this book can readily identify someone, an earlier chief executive for whom we worked, who fulfilled the mentor role and contributed significantly to whatever we later achieved.

But to some extent this is an accidental process in comparison with the other ways of helping that we discuss in this chapter. Can you create a mentor now if you don't already have one, for example because you have only just joined local government?

Very possibly someone from your earlier career experience may be able to fill part of the role for you: a management example, perhaps, which you seek to emulate and which is imported by you as added value into the local government way of doing things. Or you may strike up a friendship with a colleague in another authority whose listening you find helpful, and who as a result can fulfil some of the role of supporter and sounding-board which an older, former superior may provide for others.

Good fortune in mentoring can provide you with a powerful ally and an important source of outlet and inspiration. Do not neglect, in time, to try to offer what you have learned and gained to others who will in due course come after you.

Action learning

Action learning is a specific and powerful technique whose original development is credited to R. W. Revans some 15 to 20 years ago. There are different approaches but typically a small number of managers – perhaps five – form a 'set' for mutual discussion of projects and problems.

The set works not with a teacher or chair in the conventional sense, but with a facilitator who assists the set to release the benefits and insights for themselves. The role of facilitator is an unexpectedly unusual and demanding one (for which we have both undertaken some training): Reg Revans himself stated in 1980 that action learning processes 'attack the inveterate hankering of the teacher to be the centre of attention'.

In a typical action learning activity the set members spend a day in relaxed and uninterrupted circumstances taking turns to put issues or problems of current significance to them before the other set members. They question, they draw out experience from within the presenting set member, but they do not advise, say what they would do or give way to anecdote. The facilitator discreetly monitors the set's adherence to these rules, tries to collect and pursue points or relevances which the exchanges should not be passing by, and checks overeagerness or intrusion into someone else's conversational space. Typically a set may meet half a dozen times or more, at intervals of a few weeks spread over several months.

Action learning is a process which can run deep, and so trust within the set and complete privacy and confidentiality are essential. Writing in 1983, R. Garralt identified four key requirements for the process to have value:

1. The problem being tackled by the learning manager has to be 'crucial' to the organisation.
2. Action learners need to be people willing to take risks to develop themselves and their organisations.
3. Learners have to have real authority to take action on the problem.
4. A system has to be set up for learning effectively.

Of course, action learning has its limitations, as any approach or technique does. An obvious one is the need for the set to 'gel' and develop quickly a level of trust sufficient to allow the exploration of issues of depth which are normally concealed, or unidentified thoughts and motivations to be exposed. At chief executive level the difficulty of achieving this within one local authority setting is avoided.

Both of us have been members of action learning sets as well as undertaking facilitator training. We have also had experience of sets with private sector members as well as a set consisting entirely of local authority chief executives. Participants need to be on similar levels within their organisation but working with private sector colleagues is extremely worthwhile and can yield great value.

Action learning will not work for everyone and for every problem but we believe it is particularly valuable for chief executives in helping to overcome the issue or problem of loneliness (see pages 37–40 in Chapter 3). With complementary set members and able facilitation, however, we can testify to the worth of the technique for us.

Networking

'Networking' is really just a convenient shorthand for using your list of friends and contacts to good advantage. They will not be confined to chief executives alone even in the context of work and you are likely to find colleagues in all sorts of areas a valuable source of experience and help from time to time. (Indeed the term was flippantly defined by a fellow employee of one of us as 'a posh way of describing people you talk to at work anyway'.)

But here we are primarily concerned with your fellow chief executive contacts with whom you can expect to discuss specifically 'chief executive issues'. Although some people will come into post as chief executives with a considerable address-book of personal contacts, that is less likely for appointees from outside local government. They, in particular, may benefit from the knowledge that there are resources of friendship and support out there in other authorities, even if they do not actually need to call on them.

SOLACE maintains lists of chief executives who have expressed themselves willing to assist on both specific issues (like the gifts and hospitality guidelines set out in Appendix 2) and in general counselling, of which current details can be obtained from the SOLACE office. In fact, however, most contacts are likely to be based on personal knowledge and respect for someone who will be helpful on whatever topic is involved.

It matters little how you build your network of contacts. There will naturally be more opportunities around your own county, or SOLACE branch, to meet colleagues in the ordinary course of work. But these are not necessarily going to prove a good source of network advice for any individual. Some people don't find SOLACE branch meetings all that convenient or relevant for them, and if they contribute to SOLACE affairs in other ways (for example by joining one of the several specialist panels) that may not contribute much to your personal network if the panel happens to do most of its work by post or fax.

As elsewhere in this book, it is the outcome or practical effect for you which matters, rather than the actual process of getting there. It's important to appreciate that SOLACE members as a group are very willing to offer practical help and advice, or even just to act as a listening post or sounding-board, because they understand your context and they understand, too, the value and reassurance that talking things through with colleagues can give.

That similarity of context obviously means that you can often avoid re-inventing the wheel for yourself by using procedures and materials from other places, but networks can give a great deal more value than that (helpful and cost-effective as such exchanges are overall). Advice, practical help, reassurance, good listening, sound opinions, encouragement, sympathy, empathy, support, comfort: they can all be appropriate words at times which we need hardly take space to define. It is to be hoped that you don't need the more personal aspects of this list very often, but most of us do need them at times.

If you subscribe at all to the notion that being chief executive can be a lonely job and that it is an endlessly varied, complex and changing job, then you are also implying the value of being able to lift the telephone when you want to talk through something for which there is either no outlet or no adequate answer within your own authority.

Don't believe that all your fellow chief executives are in total command all of the time: they aren't, but they know the importance of trying to convey that impression by using their presentational skills to the full! It's normal for all of us to have doubts and difficulties.

Within your own authority you use all the reserves and resources of value to you as you judge you need them. The same ought to be true of a unique additional resource outside.

Time management

The standard joke about meaning to do a time management course but never getting around to it simply points up the truism that some of us are a lot more organised than others.

'Organised', at any rate, by the definition of being prepared and documented for every occasion, with a tidy desk and a methodically planned and maintained diary. But unfortunately, while you need a certain amount of this for obvious reasons, being methodically planned isn't the be-all-and-end-all of chief executive success or even much of a pointer towards it.

In Chapter 2 (page 25) we spoke of the importance of taking control of your diary so far as you can, and in Chapter 3 (page 43) of the value of recording things like the amounts of your extra hours or leisure time to help you realise and appreciate your commitments and overall lifestyle. Both of these topics are important background to the overall questions about ownership of your time, making space for life and health outside local government, and prioritising your working hours to make sure you attend to the essentials.

As a chief executive you have to accept that in some respects – indeed quite a lot of respects – you cannot in reality have the last word on diary commitments or the priorities you set. Appendix 4 is an example of the kind of day which can appear from nowhere in an apparently clear diary space when you meant to 'get on with some real work'. The endless shifts and requirements of the job mean that your planning must be planning for flexibility with some built-in allowances for the unexpected (or rather, the expected but unidentified!).

Within reason, because you are inevitably setting an example, you can choose your personal work style, and develop its implications with your personal staff, who become accustomed to receiving dictation tapes after you've been on a long journey, or to your preference for breakfast meetings. (We spoke on page 30 in Chapter 2 about things like starting early and finishing late, etc.) Yet again the key point is not which style or pattern you adopt but that you do consciously adopt one. That helps you to cover the ground and be prepared for the surprises, and helps others understand better how you can work together more effectively and efficiently. People will soon learn not to call on Tuesday mornings if that's your management team day, or will discover that at 5 o'clock, before committees start, you generally have a few minutes spare to talk over a cup of tea.

Use whatever tricks work for you. No pocket computer or filofax will be of the slightest help unless you use it and maintain it and that takes a certain discipline in itself.

> Faced with time constraints, C.Ex often used to choose the seemingly inessential or lower priority tasks first. This was on the basis that he would ultimately have to complete the key priorities against the deadlines (sitting up late at night if necessary), and would find the effort necessary to achieve this. He knew he would simply not be able to do this for inessentials, so finishing them first could be a deliberate means – at a price – of finding a way of making time to complete them.

One of us is a particular advocate of an answer phone and fax machine at home. These facilities guard free time and also give the flexibility to handle issues at convenient times.

By all means undertake a time management course if it is well spoken of and you feel you could learn techniques which will help you to get better use of your days: after all, whatever job we hold or the size of our authority, we all have the same number of hours in a day (and very similar holidays). You may get more out of them if you take deliberate note first of what you are doing, and that in itself will help you to help yourself.

Chapter 7

Some frequent dilemmas

- Manoeuvring
- The chief officer who wants my job, or is too close to a politician
- Civic and religious attendances
- Who fixes the agenda?
- How close do I get to my leader?
- How do I allocate goodies?
- Handling customer complaints without undermining procedures
- The chief officer with a vested interest in privatisation
- Should I go to party group meetings?
- My personal publicity profile
- Should I be the monitoring officer?
- Should I advise on standing orders and go to council meetings?
- My predecessor is still around
- Should I publish management team minutes?
- Should I live in the area?

Some themes and problems regularly recur when chief executives talk together about their work and the issues it raises. This chapter considers 15 such areas of dilemma by way of example. The order in which they appear is not significant but each of the dilemmas is real in the sense that it was put forward in November 1993 by a group of chief executives of four to five years' experience.

This is, perhaps, the right point to comment briefly on the issue of ethics and ethical dilemmas generally for chief executives. In the USA, the ICMA (see page 8) has elevated the subject of ethics for its several thousand members to a vigorous demand for a behavioural standard considered not only appropriate but necessary for city managers. A special committee considers alleged violations, and in serious cases people can lose their membership.

In the UK the term is not very popular, and SOLACE does not have a formal disciplinary mechanism analogous to its American counterpart. There is, however, rightly still an expectation and requirement for high standards of personal integrity in all aspects of a chief executive's work and lifestyle. SOLACE is willing to advise any member presented with difficulties in deciding what is 'the right and proper thing to do' in any circumstance.

Manoeuvring

The nature of local government, and in particular local politics, means that there is a great deal of wheeling and dealing, to-and-fro jockeying for position and good old-fashioned intrigue. Where there are hung councils or other special factors the scope for the making and breaking of confidences and alliances is increased.

Many chief executives, considering themselves plain-speaking, straight-forward people rather than devious or duplicitous, find that what until recent years we might have called the 'smoke-filled rooms' aspect of what goes on locally does not appeal to them. Indeed they feel not only uncomfortable but professionally endangered by being drawn into secrets and factions from which, as apolitical servants of the whole council, they would rather remain apart. That is understandable. But elsewhere in this book (see e.g. pages 26–7 and 68–9) we have referred to the necessity of understanding your authority and its political environment, and of assessing the political realities of the day. One of those realities is that to be successful you have to operate in a way which is conducive to success locally.

So you have to be streetwise about how to achieve your results and you have to be a tactician. Much negotiation and persuasion depends on choosing your moment. Not to use common sense, all the skills available to you and a little psychology to boot would hardly amount to doing your best to achieve goals which are not purely personal in the selfish sense, but goals for the overall good ultimately of the whole authority. Nevertheless, there will probably be times when you are spending more time than you would like managing the members (see pages 68–75) or the political processes, and feel more like a kind of municipal conjuror or juggler than a head of a paid service.

There is accordingly a great difference between the beneficial use of skills on the one hand to get the best out of people and possibilities, and unprofessional or unethical dealing on the other. It takes considerable and finely tuned skills to work within a complex tangle of moving relationships and interests, but to do so is manoeuvring in the context of adroit professional leadership and judgement rather than anything underhand.

A good test in any situation of this kind is to ask yourself whether either you feel in control and the manoeuvring is serving your game plan, or whether you feel you are being used in someone else's plan. If the latter, it's a sign that you may need to take some different or precautionary action to protect your own position.

The chief officer who wants my job, or is too close to a politician

There is nothing unusual or wrong in a chief officer wanting to be either *the*, or elsewhere *a*, chief executive: it's the natural step of ambition which you have probably made yourself. Sometimes, however, a chief officer oversteps the acceptable ambitions of his or her own career and appears to be actively campaigning to undermine your own position as chief executive – and perhaps even directly to oust you from office.

Personal rivalries and jealousies are amongst the most difficult human relations problems for any manager to solve, and that difficulty is compounded if you are one of the parties yourself. Only you can decide how to react, and indeed whether to appear to react at all. Bearing in mind what was said in the previous section about the wisdom of choosing your moment, you may not want to confront the situation directly for the time being.

Whatever conscious action or reaction you choose, it is important to think it through carefully in advance, weighing the possible outcomes and consequences. Try to make sure that whatever action you take gives you the best chance of reaching or retaining a position of strength. You should have an inherent advantage here by virtue of the ultimate seniority of your post, and the fact that it is not an admirable characteristic to be seen to be acting disloyally to one's superiors. Remember too that it may be a mistake to see the situation solely in terms of 'kill or be killed' interpersonal conflict. Maybe in the long run the authority will not comfortably hold both of you: in the shorter term the goal is to underline your position and try to persuade the chief officer concerned to accept theirs. How well you are seen to achieve this – if the issue is at all public – may in itself say something about the aspirations of your problem colleague. Talking things through with a chief executive from another authority or with your ALACE trade union may also be very helpful.

The chief officer who becomes too close to a politician presents different kinds of problems, which in themselves also turn to some extent on which politician and party is involved.

Probably you are going to have to take this chief officer aside to point out the dangers and difficulties. For one thing, the chief officer holds a politically restricted post as defined in section 2 of the Local Government and Housing Act 1989.

If the politician is not from a controlling party it is not difficult to illustrate how his or her position and respect will be eroded to the point where confidence may be lost altogether. And not only is this a likely member opinion, colleagues will be reluctant to be drawn into the inappropriate association if they see that as potentially compromising themselves. Furthermore, if the chief officer is weakened the whole department is weakened, with consequences for efficiency and employee morale which as chief executive you cannot afford to ignore.

Not only that, but in a party politically-organised council the administration will be quick to see leaks and conspiracies (even when they aren't really there). This could potentially quickly compromise your whole management team, if the administration feel that their confidentiality is threatened and so performance and progress towards approved council policies is being slowed or suborned.

Different connotations arise where the politician is a member, and perhaps a leading member, of the controlling administration. Charges of political partiality will come from the opposition and you may feel that your position, and that of your management team, is undermined by a chief officer colleague whose motives are different from what they should be. It is extremely difficult for a chief executive or management team if they feel that their advice is somehow being countered or shadowed in some way by an unseen commentary from another source. In some cases the party group themselves may help to resolve matters because of the dangers from their point of view of being seen to be too close to the officers and thereby too dependent on them, or perhaps because of jealousies within the group. Sometimes it is best practice, directly or indirectly, to enlist group discipline in a case you cannot really control yourself.

Whichever way round, this is not likely to be a problem you can leave alone for too long.

Civic and religious attendances

We talked about civic duties on pages 70–1 in Chapter 5. We echo here what we have already said. You may not particularly like being a dignitary but it is a status which will be largely dictated for you by the civic profile and context of your authority.

From the earlier pages you will already know we take the view that the value of the civic side is often underestimated. You may not think that dealing with it well is particularly important (a few even feel that it somehow compromises their image as a serious manager), but not to do it well is almost certain to lose you a lot of points. Many more than just a few members attach great importance to the civic life of their communities, unfashionable as it may have been in recent years, and some members obviously enjoy their civic occasions as one of the comparatively few perks of elected office. So even if you don't regard civic activities as real management or your most rewarding aspect of the job, remember that it's not a good idea to appear to be out of sympathy with what your employers regard as an important part of the job. This was brought home to one of us – Roger Morris at Northampton – who thought that he took a genuine and reasonable level of interest in the civic side but nevertheless was surprised one year to find a key performance review point from members being that he should give more emphasis to the civic side of his job as chief executive *and town clerk*. Civic duties of a religious nature can perhaps be regarded differently from other civic duties, because they obviously involve matters of personal conscience to a degree to which you are not entitled in your known views on the rest of your employer's activities.

In today's climate, with a more ecumenical outlook and a less autocratic established church approach to religious matters, it is perhaps easier for most people to meet and resolve some of the problems, particularly of an interdenominational character, than it might once have been. The common fact of a God-fearing outlook may compromise differences.

There are still difficulties, however, where compromise is not possible or, indeed, if you are an atheist with no wish to join in any form of religious observance. These still underpin many aspects of civic activities, from Remembrance Sunday and analogous civic Sundays to funerals, prayers before council meetings and even grace before meals. Can you be a chief executive and still opt out of, or fail to observe, these things?

We think the answer is yes, but it would be both fair and sensible to make your position clear at the outset (even before appointment, because an atheist ought not to be excluded from being chief executive by any authority with an equal opportunities policy). If you are going to make a stand, your authority is entitled to know *where* you stand. You must also be consistent. As this is, rather unusually in a work context, a stance based on your private or personal outlook, it is prudent to apply it evenly. A willingness to join other types of occasion with a religious element will quickly persuade your authority that a supposed personal principle is really no more than an excuse for avoiding civic duties (and thereby probably requiring someone else to stand in on your behalf).

You might also reflect that chief executives must do, and turn up to, many things in the nature of their employment which, precisely because of the apolitical nature of the job, they are not necessarily regarded as endorsing in a private capacity. While these are not the same as religious beliefs, you may feel able to attend – and thereby 'endorse' – certain values which you share with those of a religious persuasion you yourself don't have.

Who fixes the agenda?

The ultimate responsibility for what does or does not go on a council or committee agenda is often the subject of argument. The council's proper officer sends out a 'summons' to attend a council meeting under paragraph 4(2)(b) of schedule 12 to the Local Government Act 1972, but this is beside the point. It is control of content, not of physical despatch, of agendas and associated papers which is at issue here. There is no single answer. Of course, this is ultimately a question of law, but we suggest you consider the following.

Agendas, like minutes and other matters, ultimately belong to, and are the tools of, the council and not its employees. The council may if it wishes make rules about the production of agendas or drafts and when and by whom they should be sent out. This power is subject to any overall legal rules about periods of notice, availability to the public and so on.

Agenda items come from a variety of sources. Some are dictated by legal requirement, for example, to consider a monitoring officer's or local ombudsman's report in certain circumstances. Others are dictated by decisions of previous meetings to have a report at the next meeting, or whatever. Others arise because of decisions taken about business which ought in any event to be discussed. This is particularly where judgement, and potentially conflict, come in.

Save in the context of urgent business a chairman has no power, and cannot alone be given power, to decide if an item should go on an agenda. But equally nor does a chief executive or other officer have power to decide this either, though (outside of specific situations of statutory obligation) the authority may in practice have conventions which are some help in deciding what is common or expected practice. It follows that, as an agenda is not an indivisible whole but a composite, the lawful authority may come from different directions in respect of different items. Thus situations cannot be avoided where you may have a difficult judgement to make in political terms about certain items and wishes, or purported instructions about whether and how they should appear. If necessary, back your decision with a courteous and explicit letter explaining your reasons; and remember the potential of section 114 of the Local Government Finance Act 1988 and section 5 of the Local Government and Housing Act 1989 (respectively, duty of the chief financial officer to warn of unlawful expenditure and duty of the monitoring officer to warn of unlawful conduct, etc.). The development and use of agendas is an important subject broader than we can cover here. You can exercise influence in a variety of ways. For example, one chief executive of a council of largely independent membership relegated to regular information bulletins a lot of agenda items 'for information' which he considered would have been a waste of time to receive and discuss in committee.

How close do I get to my leader?

We have already written about the crucial chief executive/leader relationship on pages 51–4 in Chapter 4 and it is not necessary to repeat that again here.

But we would also draw attention to our comments on pages 68–75 in Chapter 5 about 'managing the members', and the wisdom of both discreetly keeping an eye on political trends and developments affecting your leading politicians, and of leaving a space of reserve between you and members. In that way you can in any event try to reduce the risk of being seen to be too close or of being compromised by someone presuming rather more than a proper professional or working relationship allows. And then there is the point put by SOLACE president John Horsnell (Isle of Wight CC) to a group of newly appointed chief executives in January 1994: 'Never stand between leadership and the limelight.'

Beware also that there can be dangers even in what seems to be a perfectly proper, highly effective professional relationship. A colleague who recently changed from one chief executive post to another, asked to explain his motivations for moving, said of his own chief executive/leader relationship: 'The rather quick and dictatorial style that we had adopted between us was getting up everybody's nose.'

How do I allocate goodies?

This may seem an unusual problem to label a dilemma. In fact, of course, the dispensing of patronage on any level can be a difficult business liable to cause jealousy and resentment on the one hand, and possessed of ethical and even corruption dangers on the other. As chief executive you have particular duties to be even-handed, to be consistent and above all to be fair and honest about what you do. People around you are likely to be particularly sensitive to what they interpret as signals of your favour (or indeed its opposite, which may be even more damaging all round). This is just another case of a situation where it pays to think quietly through the consequences before you commit yourself to your actions.

What exactly do we mean by 'goodies' in this context? They may take many forms (not the least insidious of which is the kind of personal privilege or favouritism that can develop around people who work around you daily). Examples include such things as:

- Opportunities to attend certain events.
- Opportunities to benefit from council hospitality, or similar sponsorship hospitality being afforded to the authority.
- Opportunities to represent or stand in for you on certain occasions, or to attend conferences.
- Opportunities to receive things like new furniture, enhanced IT facilities or whatever.
- Opportunities to receive your discretionary grant of benefits like car or telephone allowances, overtime, free parking, training places, etc.
- Opportunities to do prestigious things, like meeting royalty or other celebrity visitors.

To some it will appear ludicrous to regard these possibilities as illustrative of some supposed class of items of perk or patronage, and that the rare opportunity to be presented on a royal walk-around has little in common with allowing overtime, or deciding which of a group of candidates is to receive council sponsorship for an MBA degree. Perhaps. But we think you will do well to be on guard against any charge of partiality in your treatment of anything to which (rightly or wrongly) those around may attach some importance even if you don't yourself. Your discretion must be professional discretion, as your advice to the council is professional advice, and not about your purely personal objectives or private agenda. It is only a small step from conferring or withholding favour (or seeming to do so) to conferring or withholding status; status is still a powerful motivator of people's actions and of organisational well-being.

In the same way it's a good idea to record invitations you yourself decline, as well as those you accept. You may be glad of the proof later if any question ever arises of undue influence or poor judgement. Appendix 2 reprints the current SOLACE guidelines on gifts and hospitality.

Handling customer complaints without undermining procedures

You will want to reserve the right to look into any council issue you care to, and a certain proportion of matters will reach you and your immediate staff directly from the public or member reference. But how can you get the right balance between taking too much on, and raising unrealistic expectations on the one hand, and being accused of lack of caring commitment on the other?

There are all sorts of factors to weigh here. In part, you need to bear in mind the kind of points we made in relation to handling negotiations on pages 66–7 in Chapter 5, about not taking things too readily out of the hands of others who may well be able to deal with them better anyway. A key step to take early in the process, particularly if you're newly appointed, is to make sure you do know what policies, procedures and standards your authority has set in such matters. One newly appointed chief executive of a smaller authority told how she discovered by chance that some considerable time previously the housing department staff had been instructed never to ring back tenants.

There's a lot of guidance about – from the local ombudsman, for example – and it pays to be able to demonstrate personal awareness of it. Furthermore, an important aspect of many local ombudsman investigations is whether you've followed your own internal procedures, even if they have weaknesses. We're not suggesting weaknesses here, of course, but if you do raise expectations of administrative standards you cannot meet personally (for example, because there are too many cases for you to give them individual attention), you have needlessly stored up trouble for yourself.

> C.Ex, head of a large insurance company, had always prided himself on taking policyholders' telephone calls personally if they asked for him and had required his subordinates to do the same. But on becoming national C.Ex he found he had to change his approach: there were so many thousand policyholders he would do nothing else if he tried to speak to all those who called.

That last private sector example may just seem like practicality and common sense inevitably reining in enthusiasm. The problem, of course, for that chief executive is that he was in danger of taking no public calls whatever in future, because he would not want to give to one what he could not give to all. Common sense had a part to play here too: he needed a new screening or selecting policy consistent with both what he could handle and what he'd set up other parts of his company to deal with.

An approach which works for us is not to create so easy a hotline to your own office that it bypasses the proper people and systems (from whom you need help to respond anyway) too easily. You don't want to become the court of appeal for every last grumble.

In addition, it's good practice to ask your colleagues, especially in other departments, to review a situation much more readily than you ask them to reverse a decision. For one thing, your basic request should be enough to trigger fresh thought anyway. And it also shows that you're open-minded. You soon find out as a chief executive (indeed as a local government officer generally) that the most seemingly clear-cut cases of injustice often turn out to have surprising other sides to them, which of course the original complainant hadn't told you about. If, after due consideration, you think you should get involved, see it through, explain yourself both to the file record and to the person who made the original decision, and make your intervention count for something which would otherwise have been lacking. That way others can judge for themselves why you made the right decision.

The chief officer with a vested interest in privatisation

In today's competitive environment, increasingly it may happen that your council may wish to consider externalisation or privatisation of some service or activity. Suppose, however, you form the view that one of your chief officer colleagues is apparently promoting and encouraging such an option for reasons of personal gain? Serious questions at once arise about the ethical position of the chief officer concerned and the mix of private and professional interest, which you cannot leave unresolved. Obviously by no means every potential buy-out or similar situation involves wrongful conduct but how can you avoid the dangers, even of allegations being made, which in the public sector would be extremely serious (and also distracting from the true merits of whatever else is going on)?

A useful starting point is the Audit Commission's *Management Paper No. 6, Management Buy-outs: Public interest or private gain?* (January 1990). The paper warns about the 'clear potential conflicts of interest within the authority as the buy-out is negotiated' (summary). The recommended first response to those conflicts is declaration of interest by the proposing employees 'as soon as the MBO looks feasible', and the paper illustrates a number of other issues likely to arise or need consideration.

Feasibility, however, will be some way down the track for most cases, and your information and concern are likely to have their origins well before that stage. If that happens, almost certainly you will want to talk through your concerns with the person or persons concerned, so that at the least there is openness between you even if publicity at that stage is inappropriate (for the council too has its interest on the other side of the potential bargains).

On whatever basis you decide is appropriate, you will probably want to share your concerns and the results of the discussions you have had with leading key members, and with the chief financial officer and monitoring officer (for whom specific statutory duties may arise). If one of these statutory officers were him or herself to be involved directly, you will have to consider whether that role is compatible with the situation that has arisen. You may also need to consider an exchange of letters with the colleagues involved, to put on record both their intentions and your official response and requirements. Both your internal and external auditors ought also to be aware of developments so that they can give any advice they wish and consider their own duties accordingly. Again we emphasise that such actions imply nothing pejorative but merely precautionary: there are too many examples of things going wrong in such situations for you not to be clear about the records you keep, the checks you make and the attitudes and decisions which follow. These not only serve the council's interest – always your prime concern – but safeguard the personal positions of colleagues affected as well. An MBO may fail and make it particularly difficult to go back afterwards to how things once were.

It may be helpful to know that there is a Centre for Management Buy-Out Research (CMBOR), based at Nottingham University.

Should I go to party group meetings?

The JNC conditions of service, and one or two earlier publications like the 1979 Boynton draft guidelines referred to as paper no. 2 on page 105, have long alluded to the political world in which chief executives must operate.

Paragraph 32 of the conditions states, under the heading 'Advice to political groups', that the chief executive

shall not be required to advise any political group of the council, either as to the work of the group or as to the work of the council, neither shall he be required to attend any meetings of any political group. This shall be without prejudice to any arrangements to the contrary which may be made in agreement with the chief executive and which includes adequate safeguards to preserve the political neutrality of the chief executive in relation to the affairs of the council.

This still seems a reasonable starting point.

We think any arguments about whether in principle chief executives may go to political group meetings with professional propriety are long past. Many have done so over the years without apparent damage to their own principles or position, and the politically restricted post rules of section 2 of the Local Government and Housing Act 1989 have done nothing to change that.

But if it is important to accept that neither the law nor some kind of professional or ethical restriction inhibit chief executive attendance, it is also important to establish that councils may decide that attendance is not appropriate for them. Further, if attendance is required or expected, it is desirable to lay down ground rules, so that it can be, and be seen to be, even-handed. We examine each of those points in the next few paragraphs.

First, it is open to each council to regulate its own affairs, and the necessary conduct of its employees, within the overall confines of the law. It is therefore perfectly competent for an authority to decide that either nobody, including the chief executive, should attend group meetings or that attendance should be confined (for example) to the chief executive and chief officers. A party group meeting is not a meeting of the authority, or within its scope, and no outsider can therefore insist on attending for any reason, even the local chief executive.

Secondly, rules of attendance: obviously these must be even-handed between different groups, including independents, but opinions will differ as to what does or does not constitute even-handedness or propriety in this respect. You would be well advised to meet any signs of difficulty by clearly setting out, and perhaps validating by formal resolution, a set of rules or guidelines which you can follow. Clearly it is far better to take the initiative in laying down what those should be rather than finding yourself defending accusations of partial political practice later.

Let us quote one specific example of varying approaches. Paragraph 8 of the Boynton guidelines referred to at the beginning of this section starts by declaring that: 'If a chief executive attends a meeting of any party political group, he should inform the leadership of the other parties on the Council.' It is reasonable enough, but it is not a universal view. Some feel it equally reasonable that a party group should be able to receive advice without necessarily the other parties being aware of either the fact of attendance or the subject under discussion. This is still fair if all parties have an equal opportunity to ask for this sort of attendance, and is the basis of paragraph 6 of the equivalent Northampton provision. The Northampton *Guidelines for Member–Employee Relations* (1993) are reprinted as Appendix 3 to this book. Some problems may arise if the guidelines are confirmed or laid down in effect by a controlling party vote in your council, but of course they are nevertheless still a valid act of decision by the authority as a whole so long as they respect the law. This kind of danger underlines the wisdom of your choosing the right time (when, you hope, no particular storm clouds have gathered around these matters) to take the initiative and suggest what you propose your own practice to be, thereby increasing the chances of a unanimous or substantial vote of support away from a politically charged atmosphere.

Two other points may be made here. One is that, though there will be some exceptions, it is generally received wisdom amongst chief executives that you should not attend a group meeting when people are present who are neither council members nor employees (save of course if some outside contributor has been deliberately invited in an advisory context, such as in the example below). Both the Boynton and Northampton guidelines adopt this approach, which is intended to forestall problems where non-councillor local party members are part of the group in question. If you decide to differ from this, you increase the need for clear guidelines locally because of the difficulties and dangers involved.

> C.Ex was asked to authorise attendance at a group meeting of an outside
> consultant the council were using. The consultant would have billed the time
> involved to his account with the council. The C.Ex ruled that the attendance
> of the consultant with another officer was in principle acceptable and within
> guidelines (other groups could have issued the same invitation), but that
> council funds could not be required to pay directly or indirectly a consultancy
> bill occasioned not by advice given to the authority as appointed, but by
> advice given to a political group. (The council could have formally resolved
> to retain the consultant to advise all groups separately and similarly, but this
> was clearly unlikely to happen in practice.)

Secondly, remember that you may want to expand your guidelines in this area to cover other sorts of issues involving sharing of information. It is quite common for one approach to be taken to pre-meeting chair briefings and another to routine constituency information being copied as a courtesy to the responsible committee chair 'in accordance with the usual practice'.

> C.Ex was appointed into a politically charged atmosphere where, following
> years of stable control, that party had now lost power by a single vote. There
> were conflicting beliefs about whether his predecessor had secretly attended
> group meetings or not, and the former administration, now in unaccustomed
> opposition, wished him to attend theirs. There were no guidelines or agreed
> procedures to fall back on. C.Ex considered the background and then
> reported to the policy committee what had happened, expressed a willingness
> in principle to attend, and asked if the council would like to give him any
> instructions or advice before he made up his mind how to respond to the
> opposition group invitation. Despite some initial storm clouds, it quickly
> became clear that the overall council wish was for attendance, and C.Ex later
> had feedback that many members privately sympathised with his dilemma
> and supported his approach. The principles of group attendance were never
> again a problem in his tenure of the post (early 1980s).

We may briefly extend this question of attending group meetings to the issue of whether it is proper for you to assist in the production of party policy or manifesto material.

These words will have widely varying connotations in different places. For some, officer involvement in the origination of party policy would be unwanted and inappropriate, quite apart from political restriction issues. In other places the context is different, and helping to develop or articulate the controlling group's policy would be seen as no more than a proper and normal aspect of the chief executive's job. It could, however, be more difficult to view the same exercise for an opposition party in the same way (hence the stipulation in paragraph 5(b) of the Northampton guidelines reprinted in Appendix 3 that the chief executive 'will not advise as to the policies which any minority party should pursue'). You are likely to find some ambivalence between equality of treatment in the sense of trying to treat all parties identically and (observing the political realities of control) saying that you would treat all administration or oppositions the same. The fact is that a controlling group will have greater expectations of what you and your fellow chief officers will do for them as opposed to minority groups.

A group of chief executives of a year or so's experience were discussing this question in January 1994 and, probably rightly choosing the latter interpreta-tion of political even-handedness, proposed the following questions as a way of talking through the propriety or acceptability of something:

- What do you mean by this activity?
- Would you do the same for any group of members?
- Is this activity interpreted as a political act in your authority, or are there any local rules about it?
- Is what's being discussed really any different from regular practices like briefing of chairs for meetings, ordinary group advice and attendance, or other recognised support services?
- Who ultimately owns or controls the activity or process you're considering?

My personal publicity profile

You have a need to make a conscious assessment of the attitude of your authority's members to publicity, and to relative profiles that you and they (and, of course, particularly the leading members) should have. The place you work in, and the events which take place (for example something which receives extensive news coverage) will greatly affect how well you become known and recognised in your area.

It's good sense to recognise that who you are and what you are is bound to affect news coverage of you or media interest generally. You are entitled to your privacy like anyone else, but if being realistic you doubt that you're going to get it, then it's better not to make yourself a hostage to fortune.

If something about your lifestyle or conduct attracts distracting and unfavourable publicity, that is very easily perceived as rubbing off on your council as well as those around you. The issue may be nothing really to do with your job, but that is hard to argue with a round-the-clock role and a visible position perceived as well-paid out of public funds. What has happened may call into question your overall sense of judgement, and it's prudent to be realistic and pragmatic about not getting the last word in the media even if privately you feel unjustly hounded and seriously misrepresented. Remember that it is small comfort for anyone to be able to write on their gravestone that they had the right of way!

But even if you don't experience what we may term 'tabloid' publicity, you are likely to find yourself frequently quoted in the press or interviewed for local radio, and becoming increasingly well known in your area. Depending upon circumstances, this may present difficulties for your partner or family or any children you have at school. Most of it will just have to be accepted as part of the package of pros and cons of being a chief executive. That fact alone underlines the value of positive press relations, a conscious effort to be seen only in a necessary or constructive light and not give the local media anything which they can, when you least expect or need it, use against you to repay what they see as your past attitude.

Regrettably today you need to have some regard for your personal safety as well, including such obvious measures as ex-directory telephone numbers and ready ability to summon help if some situation becomes threatening. This must not be out of proportion but it is only prudent to apply to yourself the sort of advice your safety advisers would give other employees in any potentially vulnerable situation.

Should I be the monitoring officer?

When the role of monitoring officer was introduced by the Local Government and Housing Act 1989, SOLACE took the overall view that it was not only appropriate but probably desirable for the chief executive to hold both the new statutory roles of head of the paid service and monitoring officer.

In March 1990 the Society arranged a survey on who were the new monitoring officers (515 forms were sent out and 438 (85 per cent) were returned). The result showed more or less an even split overall as follows:

Type of authority	Chief executive	Other posts (essentially chief legal post)
English county	15	20
English metropolitan	13	15
English district	121	136
London borough	12	14
Scottish region	1	8
Scottish district	23	21
Welsh county	4	4
Welsh district	17	14
TOTAL	206	232
Percentage	47%	53%

Some years on, we think it probable that the proportion of chief executives who hold the monitoring officer role will have declined slightly, and that the number who think it unimportant or unhelpful to hold it is probably rather higher than 50 per cent. Nevertheless, the holding of either view obviously is or remains compatible with the chief executive role.

But what about the practical considerations? Do you want the monitoring role, or might it be at best an irrelevance and at most a hindrance for you?

In a smaller authority, particularly if you happen to be legally qualified, a significant factor may be the limited number of alternatives, granted that the same person cannot be head of the paid service, monitoring officer and chief financial officer together. And it may also be significant that chief executives with a legal or (town) clerk's background tend both to identify themselves, and to be identified, with the monitoring role more readily than others.

You have to ask yourself about your priorities. Your chief executive role is paramount: will being monitoring officer help that role or not? Might it actually get in the way by requiring you to fulfil statutory (and inherently unwelcome) duties – worthy though they are in themselves – when you would rather be using your chief executive skills to deal with the problems in other ways? Like reading small print, it is important to imagine yourself in a scenario of difficulty and dilemma over the statutory duties, rather than in an uncontroversial routine situation. In such a case, may you not welcome the additional dimension and support which another colleague may give, and the opportunity to use the inevitability of the monitoring officer's independent powers as a lever to achieve progress through the problems which you might not otherwise have the flexibility to use?

It might be more difficult to decide this at the start of your service as chief executive, simply because (unless you are an internal appointment) it is less easy to discern the relevant context, and any prior history of formal use of monitoring officer powers, etc. If you cannot establish the situation, and make your choice to your satisfaction on day one, remember that later on it will probably be much easier to shed the monitoring role than to take it over from someone else.

A survey of the scope and frequency of formal monitoring officer reports by John Barber and Roger Morris was published in *Local Government Chronicle* on 18 June 1993 (pp. 16–17) under the title 'A muddle over monitors'. In 307 responding authorities there had been 82 such reports (covering a very wide range of subjects) in 40 authorities over the first three years that the statutory provisions had been in force.

Should I advise on standing orders and go to council meetings?

This issue is partly akin to the previous monitoring officer question, but is different. Whereas monitoring is a statutory role, 'taking' council meetings or being the adviser of the chair on the conduct of meetings and standing orders is much more a matter of local tradition within each authority.

In many, if not most, authorities, the full council meeting is a formal and rather inflexible affair quite unlike most committee business. Advising on standing orders in the heat of debate is an acquired skill. It may be more easily learnt by lawyers and administrators than others, but there is no reason why others should not handle it equally successfully after a little practice.

However, some feel this sort of thing is not only an acquired skill but an acquired taste, and one redolent with a municipal past that has nothing in common with their own priorities or management style. That is a perfectly defensible and professional viewpoint.

Think through the practical consequences and any signals you may give, if you decide *not* to carry out this role. Who *will* do it? Will there be any overtones of power, influence or status associated with that which you do not want or intend?

Remember also that key interventions in meetings are often about real substance, and not just about procedure. To be out of whisper-reach of the chair is to be significantly removed from a pivotal position of influence. So if you are not going to be the standing orders adviser, make your positioning and your reasoning clear at the outset. Make sure also that mechanistic things like where you sit, and whether you can speak anyway, are clear and adequate for your needs, for otherwise full council meetings might be a regular public display of your apparent limitations and marginalising rather than your role as principal policy adviser.

For that reason, regular attendance at full council meetings is probably prudent, even if you think them unnecessary for your priorities and see them as a time-taking chore. Members are apt to think that if they ought to go, so should you!

My predecessor is still around

Perhaps early retirements increase the tendency: anyway, SOLACE meetings and other activities often have a proportion of retired colleagues present.

Many sitting tenants find this uncomfortable or inappropriate. The problem is compounded if their own predecessor is active and still living locally, and makes a habit of coming to council events and generally being in regular contact with members and others.

For one thing it can give a successor an uncomfortable feeling of insecurity to feel – even if unjustifiably – that his or her predecessor is effectively still advising, commenting and networking. It is also an unwanted extra personal issue to handle if you have been appointed to – or have decided to – make radical changes which of necessity or by implication are going to be read as critical of your predecessor. Probably the best approach is to rely on your self-confidence to draw a line across your predecessor's reign, avoid harking back to it as much as possible, and simply move on. The speed of things today means that people recede into the distance quicker than you often expect. New employees and members arrive who don't recall your predecessor's tenure and can't make comparisons anyway. Time sorts things out.

If necessary, if it is inhibiting you, you may have to confront this issue as you would any other people problem within the authority. With a combination of courtesy, tact and firmness you have to tell your predecessor that you need some space, and that things have moved on. You will also have to see if you can neutralise some of any unwelcome advice or influence which you think is cramping your style.

You will also need to remember how you feel now when the day comes for you to have a successor!

Should I publish management team minutes?

For most of us, two key principles are likely to govern the answer to this issue. The first is the importance of employees in the authority knowing clearly who comprise the management team, what that team is supposed to be doing, and what lead it's giving on the various strategies or matters being discussed.

The second is the need to be sensitive to the political realities of the authority, and the fact that management team members, collectively and individually, are serving the whole council and not just a particular administration. This may well mean that some matters, or parts of them, have perforce to remain confidential.

This need for confidentiality, when it arises, is not a powerful argument for publishing nothing at all of the rest of the business. This is another of the many cases where a sensible balance has to be struck, including the extent to which these meetings are revealed to members. It would be sensible to avoid a situation where only one political party had access to management team minutes.

We define management team here as an officer meeting. It is hard to see how you could sensibly operate without the regular opportunity of discussions without member attendance, even if members are frequently part of the overall process. It may be helpful to rely on your head of the paid service statutory duties under the Local Government and Housing Act 1989 in the event of difficulty on this score. It may also be a matter on which there should be clearly developed practices and understandings on all sides: see pages 22–3 and Appendix 3.

Should I live in the area?

Authorities vary so much in size and topography that a straight answer to this kind of question is impossible. Nobody expects most employees of the London boroughs to live in the one they work for. Equally, someone may be two miles from the office but in another authority's district. Indeed, some authorities actually have offices outside their own areas.

Chief executives vary in their views on whether you must live in the area to be, and to look like you're being, part of the community, or whether you may or should live outside to give yourself some space and escape from the pressure of feeling that everything faintly municipal you see around you is somehow down to you to fix or be responsible for. We think a majority both believe they ought to, and do, live in their authority's areas, but it is uncertain that any 'typical' or 'average' view would mean much in this either/or sort of debate. No formal research seems to have been done into the proportion of chief executives who live in the area for which they work.

Vital, of course, is the attitude of your authority, who may well stipulate from the outset that the successful candidate must live in the area. But if it would be foolish to ignore a clear wish or signal, it would be unwise also not to test out your intentions at the start if your arrangements might be considered at all unusual.

Energetic weekend commuting for a while, for instance, may be unavoidable and the authority will probably be helping with the consequent costs. But to live far away for good without clear approval is likely to be badly received by many councils, quite apart from the difficulties it brings over civic and other weekend commitments, emergency availability and so on. If anything else prompts member dissatisfaction, it is all too easy for them to quote your distant home address, begin to quote that as lack of commitment to their area, and *that* in turn as a reason for justifying your departure.

Yet again you need to recognise what signals you may be giving, and then take a few common-sense steps to keep yourself on side.

Chapter 8

What else has been written?

- Books
- Other materials

Remarkably little, certainly in any lasting form, was published about the role of the chief executive for some years. Since the middle of the 1980s that has changed considerably, though the Bains report (see page 14) was almost 20 years old before there was a study of the chief executive more or less parallel in intent to the classic 1962 study by T. E. Headrick of *The Town Clerk in English Local Government* (George Allen and Unwin). (Commissioned by the trustees of the former Society of Town Clerks, Alan Norton is currently writing a new study provisionally entitled *The Town Clerk: The nature of the role and its contribution to British local government*.)

Books

Three books dedicated to the role have been published in recent years, all of them quoted earlier in these pages.

First in the field in 1986 was Sir John Boynton with *Job at the Top: The chief executive in local government* (Longman). In 1991 was published Alan Norton's study of *The Role of Chief Executive in British Local Government: Its origins and development, present reality and future*. Published by INLOGOV through the imprint of the University of Birmingham, Norton's book was commissioned by SOLACE and sponsored by the Royal Institute of Public Administration and that Society. It is a full-length serious academic study for which substantial questionnaire research was carried out (263 chief executives responded out of 504 canvassed).

Alan Norton's study was followed in 1993 by a very readable privately initiated book on *The Role of Chief Executives in Local Government* (Longman) by Professor Janice Morphet. This is unique in providing a picture (based also on a substantial questionnaire response) drawing on the author's own practical experience as a chief officer (at the time director of technical services at Woking Borough Council).

These three books differ greatly, and are meant to be used in different contexts. Taken together, they provide a valuable blend of views and insights, though the world of local government they portray is already changing.

Other materials

The following papers, which are listed below in order of publication as far as can be ascertained, are just a small selection of the rapidly increasing literature available. We have chosen these largely because of either their immediate relevance to the themes of this book or the fact that they have themselves been written from an inside viewpoint by serving chief executives. We concentrate here, as elsewhere in this book, not on service delivery issues but on the being, feeling and doing side of what being a chief executive is about.

Some of SOLACE's earlier occasional papers, generally commissioned via what is now the Human Resources Panel and its predecessors, were undated and unsigned. A different approach usually applies today, particularly in the fruitful collaboration with the Local Government Management Board (LGMB, formerly the Local Government Training Board).

1. *Recruitment and Training of Chief Executives*, 1977, SOLACE Occasional Paper.
2. *The Chief Executive and Party Politics in Local Government*. Guidelines from a Policy Studies Institute and RIPA seminar on 24 May 1979, drafted by Sir John Boynton, published as pp. 48–50 of *Party Politics in Local Government: Officers and members* by those bodies, 1980. Currently also published as Appendix B to Chapter 1 of the ICSA *Local Government Administrator's Manual*.
3. *Management Development and the Chief Executive*, SOLACE Paper 7 reporting a seminar in May 1982, and published jointly by SOLACE and LGTB.
4. *The Salary Structure for Chief Executives and Chief Officers in Local Government: A consultative paper*, November 1983, Local Authority Conditions of Service Advisory Board (LACSAB).
5. *Leadership in Local Government*, August 1984, LGTB.
6. *Training Needs of the Newly Appointed Chief Executive*, c.1985, SOLACE Occasional Paper.
7. *Communication*, c.1985, SOLACE Occasional Paper.
8. *Five Years Plus*, c.1985, SOLACE Occasional Paper written by Roger Morris about issues for chief executives who have been in post for five years or more.
9. *The Role of the Chief Executive: Implications for training and development*, December 1986, a paper for SOLACE by Michael Clarke and Professor John Stewart published jointly by SOLACE and LGTB.
10. *A Survey of the Background and Responsibilities of Local Authority Chief Executives*, undated (1987), JNC for Chief Executives.

11. *A Profile of Chief Executives and Their Jobs*, March 1985, JNC for Chief Executives.

12. *More Equal Than Others: The chief executive in local government*, January 1989, Audit Commission Management Paper No. 2.

13. *Getting Started: The experience of newly appointed chief executives.* Report of conference at Grosvenor House Hotel, London on 12 April 1989, published jointly by SOLACE, LGTB and Korn/Ferry International.

14. *Recruiting and Selecting a Chief Executive: Guidelines for good practice*, 1989, SOLACE Occasional Paper, published jointly by SOLACE and LGTB.

15. *Political Leadership in Local Government*, 1990, an LGTB paper written by Steve Leach and Professor John Stewart.

16. *The Role of the Chief Executive*, April 1991, by Michael Clarke and John Stewart, published by LGMB.

17. *Chief Executives' Development (for Effectiveness)*, April 1992, a questionnaire-based study prepared by the SOLACE Human Resources Panel and LGMB (sponsored by KPMG Management Consulting).

18. *Chief Executives' Development Survey*, July 1992, a questionnaire-based study prepared by the SOLACE Human Resources Panel and LGMB.

19. *Leadership and Quality Management: A briefing note for chief executives and senior managers*, 1992, written by Noorzaman Rashid with contributions from Roger Letch, published by LGMB.

20. *Chief Executives' Development Survey*, February 1993, a study of local authority chief executives' career patterns, jobs, development needs and their authorities' performance management systems, published jointly by SOLACE and LGMB.

21. *Shaping the Organisation and Management of Local Authorities – Challenges and Issues for the Nineties*, March 1993, paper published by LGMB.

22. *Managing Tomorrow: Panel of inquiry report*, April 1993, published by LGMB.

23. *The Local Authority Chief Executive: 'A good one makes a change'*, May 1993, SOLACE Occasional Paper.

24. *Looking for Direction: Checklist for chief executives-designate of new unitary authorities created as a result of local government review*, undated (1993), published by LGMB.

25. *Fitness for Purpose: Shaping new patterns of organisation and management*, undated (1993), published by LGMB.

26. *After Early-Retirement: A practice note*, Edition 1, December 1993, written by Roger Jefferies and published by ALACE.

27. *The Partnership in Interim Management for Local Authorities*, undated (March 1994), published by SOLACE and PE Interim Management.

28. *Commissioning the New Authorities*, June 1994, published jointly by SOLACE and LGMB.

29. *Code of Conduct for Local Government Employees* (corrected print September 1994), published by AMA, ADC, ACC and LGMB.

30. *Appointing a Chief Executive: Advice for members on the recruitment process*, undated (December 1994), published by LGMB (and also in summary form).

31. *Local Government Chronicle and Newchurch and Company Survey of Chief Executives 1994* (April 1995), the report of *Taking the Pulse of Local Government*, a survey of local authority chief executives, taken in November 1994.

Appendix 1

Defining competencies

Pages 6–9 in Chapter 1 discuss the importance of competencies in current attitudes to preparation for, and fulfilment of, the role of chief executive. SOLACE has been working alongside others to develop a competency profile. To give an idea of what this kind of approach is about, the following is extracted from a draft profile provisionally adopted for questionnaire purposes at the Society's Human Resources Panel meeting in October 1992, starting with the competency groupings:

1. Relationship with others.
2. Interpersonal communication.
3. Focused on results.
4. Team management.
5. Managing political relationships.
6. Self-confidence, stress and self-management.
7. Corporate perspective.
8. Intellect.
9. Decision-making.
10. Organisational commitment.
11. Change management.
12. Strategic management.
13. Influencing skills.

1. Relationship with others

- Forges purposeful, trusting relationships with others.
- Relates to all levels of staff and gains their support.
- Makes opportunities to meet and talk with a wide variety of people.
- Uses praise to acknowledge achievements of others.
- Is willing to confront difficult personal situations/poor performance.

2. Interpersonal communication

- Prefers to communicate face-to-face.
- Can clearly articulate ideas and issues.
- Uses concise, jargon-free language.
- Listens to others' views and ideas.
- Gives feedback to others.

3. Focused on results

- Displays a personal drive/enthusiasm to make things happen.
- Uses objectives to focus behaviour (personal and organisational).
- Develops clear priorities.
- Sees things through to the end.

4. Team management

- Builds effective team relationships in senior management team.
- Gains an understanding of the strengths and weaknesses of the senior management team.
- Helps the senior management team to recognise individual and collective responsibilities.

5. Managing political relationships

- Actively develops effective, communicative relationships with politicians (especially leading politicians).
- Gains the trust, confidence and respect of politicians.
- Assists politicians to develop and prioritise strategic objectives for the council.
- Successfully influences politicians by presenting alternative proposals, ideas or additional information.

6. Self-confidence, stress management and self-management

- Demonstrates self-confidence in actions, own abilities and relationships.
- Clearly and willingly articulates an opinion.
- Demonstrates sound self-knowledge.
- Is able to deal with uncertainty.
- Is able to maintain performance when under pressure/stress.
- Successfully balances many competing demands.

7. Corporate perspective

- Views all issues against the wider corporate interest, priorities and context.

- Identifies linkages and parallels between ideas and issues across service areas.
- Focuses on management issues, not technical issues.
- Uses professional/technical background to enhance options not limit them.
- Demonstrates a wide knowledge of local government services.

8.   Intellect

- Can quickly and accurately identify key issues.
- Demonstrates well-developed analysis skills.
- Able to grasp and deal with a number of complex issues at once.
- Generates appropriate solutions to problems.

9.   Decision-making

- Is willing to make 'sole' decisions.
- Often generates solutions through consultation.
- Gathers information from a wide variety of sources to inform decisions.
- Establishes a balance between not enough (broad-brush) and too much (detailed) information, to meet requirements.
- Organisational priorities inform decision-making.
- Communicates reasons for decisions, not just the decision.

10.   Organisational commitment

- Demonstrates a longer-term commitment to the job, the organisation, the community and to local government in general.
- Actively promotes and enhances the authority's public image.
- Is comfortable with a publicly visible role.

11.   Change management

- Constantly seeks new and improved ways of doing things.
- Is proactive in seeking, promoting and effecting change.
- Attempts to maintain a momentum in change efforts.
- Actively seeks to identify opportunities for the authority.
- Takes calculated risks.
- Is able to generate fresh, innovative ideas to address problems.
- Encourages the development of new ideas from all levels of staff.
- Uses new ideas to inform decisions.
- Constantly monitors and reviews things.
- Can identify when things are going wrong and put them right.

12. Strategic management

- Has a clear 'vision' for the organisation.
- Clearly and consistently communicates organisation purpose and direction down the organisation.
- Scans the external and internal environments in order to identify future issues which may affect the organisation.
- Makes decisions with a longer-term view.
- Encourages chief officers to think strategically.
- Seeks feedback to ensure organisation mission/vision is being achieved.

13. Influencing skills

- Uses personal energy and enthusiasm to motivate staff and gain commitment.
- Is willing to influence.
- Gains the confidence of others.
- Is persuasive and timely in the presentation of ideas and options to others.
- Focuses on gaining the support of 'key' people/develops coalitions when necessary.

Page 8 in Chapter 1 also refers to the 27 'practices' (as they prefer to call them) identified as important to the profession of local government management by respondents to the 1992 ICMA postal survey of their own membership, the *Dialogue on the Profession*. The 27 were reported as follows:

- Personal integrity.
- Facilitating council or board effectiveness.
- Quality of results.
- Budget.
- Team leadership.
- Delegating.
- Financial analysis.
- Empowerment.
- Strategic planning.
- Functional area of expertise.
- Citizens service.
- Vision.
- Facilitative leadership.
- Systematic thinking.
- Initiative and risk taking.
- Diversity.
- Presentation skills.
- Negotiation/mediation.
- Local democracy.

- Creativity and innovation.
- Media relations.
- Operational planning.
- Citizen participation.
- Coaching/mentoring.
- Responsible followership.
- Advocacy.
- Public/private partnership.

The ICMA Task Force analysed these results during 1993 and subsequently published the following summary in volume 1, no. 6 of the international edition of the *ICMA Newsletter* (November–December):

1. Dialogue results showed that after 'personal integrity', the other practices (previously called 'competencies') received similar ratings regarding level of importance. Rather than trying to extract a 'core', the task force recommended that the practices be grouped under descriptive headings for the purpose of developing continuing education activities.
2. The dialogue showed that the majority of the membership supported personal assessment, professional development activities and some type of recognition for professional development.

   Members also agreed that professional organisations should do more to identify and provide educational resources, but should not monitor or require activities. The task force recommended that specific voluntary roles be identified for the individual member, state and affiliate organisations, and ICMA with regard to providing or pursuing ongoing professional development. (While the task force and facilitators would like to see some demonstration of ICMA members actively engaged in ongoing professional development activities, they chose to honour the feedback from the Dialogue in developing these recommendations.)

ICMA's follow-up questionnaire and development work on these themes continues and the results of the *Dialogue on the Profession* Survey II were published in the subsequent international editions of the *Newsletter*, with an article (pp. 8–9 of no. 2) on the acceptance of the report by the ICMA Executive Board in January 1994 (volume 2, nos 1 and 2, January–February and March–April 1994 respectively).

Appendix 2

SOLACE guidelines on gifts and hospitality

The Society of Local Authority Chief Executives (SOLACE) agreed in 1990 the following advice note for its members on the acceptance or otherwise of gifts and hospitality (see also page 92 in Chapter 7).

General

The creation of good external relations both inside and outside a council's area is one of the prime responsibilities of a chief executive so a chief executive will inevitably be faced with the difficulty of deciding whether or not to accept gifts and hospitality. Whilst it is impossible to cover every set of circumstances, the following guidelines should provide a basis for making a decision in the vast majority of cases.

The general approach of the prime minister's Committee on Local Government Rules of Conduct to the problems of gifts and hospitality is expressed:

> Another particular source of conflict between the private and public interest is the offer of gifts, hospitality or other benefits in kind to councillors in connection with their official duties. A nice exercise of judgement may sometimes be necessary to decide how the public interest, and the authority's good name, may be best served. A reasonable amount of entertainment is a normal part of the courtesies of public life and extreme strictness can give unnecessary offence to people and organisations with whom the authority's relationships should be cordial. But an appearance of improper influence is easily created and with it encouragement of cynicism about the motives of those who serve in local government.

In applying the judgement, chief executives are strongly advised to err on the side of caution and to consult if they are in any doubt in a particular case.

These guidelines are intended primarily for chief executives who, nevertheless, should ensure that staff are given clear instructions on this subject. Staff at lower levels will often run the greater risk of their actions being misinterpreted simply because they are often in a much closer working relationship with donors. There should be arrangement in each department for staff to report to their superior the offer of any gifts or hospitality and there should be a record in log form or by letter of thanks for any gifts or hospitality. It is considered best practice to finalise any arrangements in writing with the donor. The guidance also applies to spouses and other close members of chief executives' families.

Gifts

The acceptance of gifts is a dangerous practice and the general rule should be to refuse tactfully all such offers from organisations or persons who do, or might, provide work, goods or services to the council, or who need some decision from the council (e.g. planning application).

Exceptions from this general rule would include modest gifts of a promotional character (for example, calendars, diaries, articles for office use, or a small gift during a courtesy visit to a firm). Such exceptions relate only to modest gifts and an expensive gift would raise questions even if it would otherwise fall within one of the above categories. It is impossible to be more precise in dealing with what do and do not amount to acceptable gifts and this is very much a matter for the individual judgement of chief executives given the particular circumstances.

Hospitality

When to accept hospitality is again very much a matter of judgement given the particular circumstances and it would be wrong to produce an atmosphere in which chief executives refuse all invitations for social involvement with persons or bodies who have, or may seek to have in the future, business dealings with the council. Contacts established at a social level can often be helpful in pursuing the council's interests. What is important is to avoid any suggestion of improper influence or giving others the opportunity reasonably to impute improper influence. The extent of the hospitality will be a factor as to its acceptability. It may be more reasonable to join in hospitality offered to a group than to accept something unique to yourself.

When a particular person or body has a matter currently in issue with a local authority then common sense dictates a more restrictive approach (for example, negotiations with an outside organisation). An important criterion in exercising your judgement is what interpretation others may reasonably put on your acceptance.

The following checklist of questions should help chief executives to decide whether a gift or an offer of hospitality should be accepted or tactfully rejected:

1. Is the donor, or event, significant in the community or in your council's area?
2. Are you expected to attend because of your position in the community?
3. Will the event be attended by others of a similar standing in the community or in other communities?
4. What is the motivation behind the invitation?
5. Would acceptance of the invitation be, in any way, inappropriate or place you under pressure in relation to any current or future issue involving your council?
6. Could you justify the decision to your council, press and public?
7. Is the extent of the hospitality or the nature of the gift reasonable and appropriate?
8. How will you respond to the hospitality?
9. Are you comfortable with the decision?

SOLACE maintains a panel of members willing to advise on difficult cases. By way of contrast, it may be useful to refer to the NHS Management Executive document of health service guidelines entitled *Standards of Business Conduct for NHS Staff* published on 18 January 1993. The Local Government Management Board (LGMB) has also published its own *Code of Conduct* (1994).

Appendix 3

Northampton guidelines for member–employee relations

The following guidelines, referred to on page 96 in Chapter 7, are not offered in any way as a model. But they may be a helpful starting point for another context. They were prepared by Roger Morris at Northampton (but in a climate where the administration had indicated that some guidelines were needed) and were then endorsed by the policy committee on behalf of the borough council on 7 April 1993.

The guidelines begin with the following introduction, signed by the chief executive:

> The chief executive and town clerk, after consultation with management team, has prepared these guidelines governing member–employee relations. No such code can be comprehensive; the intention is to provide a framework within which relationships can be continued in a proper manner which respects the different roles of the participants as well as recognising the statutory requirements and standing orders of the council.
>
> The chief executive and town clerk will advise on any matters referred to him.

The guidelines themselves are in the following terms:

The chief executive and town clerk

1. The chief executive and town clerk is the employee of the council as a whole and his overriding responsibility is to the council and not to any party political group.
2. The chief executive and town clerk is nevertheless expected to work closely with the administration for the time being and to give them information, assistance and advice. Subject to maintaining his position as politically neutral he may develop a special relationship with the administration

leadership and will not without consent disclose to the minority parties any matters discussed with that leadership.

3. The political neutrality of the chief executive and town clerk should be respected by everyone. He should not be asked to play any role or undertake any task which is likely to prejudice that neutrality or make it difficult for him to serve a different majority political party at some future time in the authority.

4. All members of the council have a right of access to the chief executive and town clerk. Where a member requires information, it will be provided if it is readily available, for example, in committee papers or material published on behalf of the council. The chief executive and town clerk is free to give advice on a confidential basis about procedural matters to any member. In doubtful cases, the chief executive and town clerk is entitled to seek the instructions of a chairman or a committee before responding to a request from a councillor.

5. The following principles govern the relationship between the chief executive and town clerk and the minority parties:

    (a) It is proper for the chief executive and town clerk to develop a working relationship with the minority parties on the council.

    (b) The chief executive and town clerk is free to provide information and answer procedural inquiries to members of any minority party as set out in para. 6. He will not advise as to the policies which any minority party should pursue.

    (c) The chief executive and town clerk will ensure that the administration leadership is aware of information provided by him to representatives of minority parties, unless it either be of a routine or trivial nature or to do so would be a breach of confidence or other statutory, formal or guideline requirement.

    (d) Because the chief executive and town clerk is the employee of the whole council, he will draw the attention of the administration leadership to any case where consideration should, in his opinion, be given to affording information, consultation or representation to the minority parties.

    In applying these principles to any given situation, the chief executive and town clerk will have regard to the perceived customs of the authority, to any established traditions, and to any statutory or accepted procedural rules governing the rights of minority parties to information, consultation or representation.

6. If the chief executive and town clerk attends a meeting of any party political group, he need not inform the leadership of the other parties on the council. He will ensure that the part he plays in the proceedings is consistent with his political neutrality. He will not attend party political group meetings at which there are persons present who are neither elected members nor officials of the authority.

Directors

The foregoing principles apply similarly to all directors, who shall act under the general direction and after seeking the advice of the chief executive and town clerk as statutory head of the paid service.

Other employees

Although the considerations applicable to management team members affect other employees differently, the most senior employees, and those additionally closely associated with the political processes, are statutorily politically restricted.

It is also the duty of the chief executive and town clerk and each director to ensure that the work and responses of employees are conducive to, and not undermining of, the foregoing general principles. They are entitled to expect members to respect political restriction and the duties and limitations of employees.

It is also the duty of the chief executive and town clerk and each director to arrange matters so that their employees properly understand the roles of members and employees and the council's required approaches to the relations between them. They are also entitled to expect members to respect the degree of seniority of employees with whom they may have dealings and the fact that, while those employees owe duties to the council as their employer, such duties are first expressed to their respective director and or the chief executive and town clerk and not to any individual member.

Appendix 4

One day in the life of a chief executive

As a chief executive you must thrive on the unexpected, cope with surprise and have a sense of humour on hand to deal with some of the more ludicrous situations or contrasts you'll come across.

The following is not a typical day, but it was a real day: actually Thursday, 15 April 1993. The narrative below, reproduced more or less in the note form in which it was contemporaneously recorded, is a microcosm of the job's endless variety and capacity to surprise. It contains the crisis blowing up without warning in a clear sky; the need to make quick, tactful and tactical judgements; the need both to investigate and to defend officer actions against unreasonable or unauthorised demands but where something has clearly gone wrong; the need to exercise wise political judgement; the absurd civic interlude punctuating the day; the need to deal with routine after the crisis has been coped with; and the staying up at night to work on essentials after official business was long over.

These were the notes of the day:

C.Ex's secretary away for Easter week: a clear day with only one minor diary commitment, which is very unusual. Second secretary suggests using the free space for some pending discussions.

By 9.30 am an angry leader is on the telephone about an unexpected item at last night's planning committee revealing an explosive and unauthorised planning application in his ward where his wife is standing in the county council elections. Disciplinary action is demanded, and a report within the day about who is responsible. After brief consideration C.Ex decides to get worst over at once, before it either gets worse still or committee or group resolutions are passed entrenching the demands. The morning is largely taken up with inquiries with the director, etc. while working on some routine correspondence, etc. Arranges a meeting of key members and officers in his office for 2 pm.

Lunch consists of visiting the leisure centre to witness a chained escapologist undo the manacles while sliding down the newly re-opened flume.

2 pm: Leader angrily demands senior officer reveals another officer's name who is allegedly at fault in causing politically motivated attempt to undermine his administration. C.Ex intervenes to protect officer's position that he should not be expected to do this. C.Ex (who members know had no prior personal knowledge of this any more than they did) accepts full managerial responsibility and apologises for what has occurred. Placates leader by promising further investigation and written conclusions (but not necessarily disciplinary action) within two working days.

Tries to conclude routine matters in rest of afternoon.

Spends evening later sitting up past midnight reading an Audit Commission paper on the client function plus CIPFA draft studies on trading accounts and the way forward for post-CCT authority structures and approaches.

Index

Accessibility 72–3, 117
Action learning 81–3
Age, average upon appointment 19
Agenda 90–1
Appointment
  act and mechanism 14–17
  average age 19
  average length of government
    service 19
  career background 20
  economic profile of area 21–2
  external local government 19–30
  external non-local government 31
  internal 17–19
    adjustment problems 18
    advantages 17–18
  preparation for 21–30
    agendas, minutes, reports etc., to
      see regularly 27–8
    checking powers, authorities etc.
      of officers 22–3
    diary for first couple of months
      25–6
    extent of civil commitments
      24–5
    getting to know people in area
      23–4
    getting to know political leaders
      24
    historical background of area 24

management approach 29–30
management structure and
  budget of authority 22
personal image projection 30
personal staff 25
personal style 28
priorities given by yourself 27
priorities given to you by
  members 26–7
Arroba, T. & James, K., *Pressure at
  Work: A survival guide* 43, 44
Assessment centres 16
Association of Local Authority Chief
  Executives (ALACE) 13, 15
Atheism 90
Audit Commission
  Management Buyouts 94
  More Equal than Others 65

Bains Report, *The New Local
  Authorities Management and
  Structure* 1, 14–15
Barber, J., *A muddle over monitors*
  100
Benefits, discretionary grant 92
Boyatzis, R., *The Competent
  Manager: A model for effective
  performance* 8
Boynton, Sir John
  guidelines on political groups 95, 96

Boynton, Sir John (*continued*)
   *Job at the Top: The chief executive
      in local government* 104
Budget process 66
Building Societies Act 1986 2

Career background 20
Chairman of council 51
Change management 110
Chief officers
   after Chief Executive's job 87–8
   politically restricted post 88
   relationship with chief executive
      57–61
   too close to politician 88–9
Church attendance 43
Civic duties 24–5, 70–1, 89
Clarke, M., *The Role of the Chief
   Executive* 65
Colleagues outside authority,
   feedback 80
Community contacts, external
   network 32–3
Community life 70–1
Competencies, defining 108–12
Competency, meaning of term 8
Conditions of service 5, 16, 17
Controlling groups, relationship with
   chief executive 55–6
Corporate body language 74
Corporate perspective 109–10
Council meeting attendance 100–1
Councillor, lack of power to bind
   council 56
Counselling service, SOLACE 13
Customer complaints 93–4

Day in life of chief executive 119–20
Decision-making 110
Delegations 16
Directors 118

Early tenure 31–4
Economic profile of area 21–2

Employees
   accessibility of chief executive 72–3
   development 67–8
   feedback 79–80
   relations 116–17
   relationship with chief executive
      61–2
Ethical dilemmas 86
Ethics 86
Experience,
   broadening 10–11
   value of 9
External local government
      appointment 19–30
External non-local government
      appointment 31

Family 42
   feedback 80
Feedback 76–81
   from colleagues outside authority
      80
   from external sources 80–1
   from family and friends 80
   from leading members 77–8
   from members 78–9
   from other employees 79–80
First impressions 74
Fixed-term contracts 15
Friends, feedback 80

Garralt, R. 82
Gifts 92
   SOLACE guidelines 113–15

Handling negotiations 66–7
Headrick, T.E., *The Town Clerk in
   English Local Government*
   104
Hospitality 92
   SOLACE guidelines 113–15
Housing Act 1988 2

Image 74

Independents, relationship with chief
    executive 56–7
Influencing skills 111
Intellect 110
Internal appointment 17–19
    adjustment problems 18
    advantages 17–18
International City-County
    Management Association
    (ICMA)
    competencies 112
    Dialogue on the profession 8–9
Interpersonal communication 109
Interview for post 16
Invitations, recording 92
Isolation 35–7, 81

Job description 15, 16–17
Joint Negotiating Committee 13
    conditions of service 5, 95

Leader of council
    relationship with chief executive
        51–4
    special responsibility allowance 52
LGMB
    *Best Practice in Management and
        Selection: A guide to the use of
        assessment centres in local
        government* 16
    *Chief Executives' Development
        Effectiveness* study 10
    *Chief Executives' Development
        Survey* 19–20
    *Continuing Professional
        Development: Partnership for
        change* 8
    *Managing Tomorrow: Panel of
        inquiry report* 6
    papers 105–7
LGTB, *Recruiting and Selecting a
    Chief Executive: Guidelines
    for good practice* 15
Living in area 102–3

Local Government Act 1955 50
Local Government Act 1972 56
Local Government Act 1986 50
Local Government Act 1989 52
Local Government and Housing Act
    1989 16, 50, 56, 99
Loneliness 37–40, 81, 82

Management approach 29–30
Management competencies 6–9
Management team minutes,
    publishing 102
Managing political relationships
    109
Manoeuvring 87
Mayor 51
Members, feedback 78–9
Members, leading, feedback 77–8
Members management 68–75
    assessment of political realities
        68–9
    remaining formal 71–2
Mentoring 81
Miles, B. & Morris, R., *Fixed-term
    Contracts for Chief Executives*
    15
Monitoring officer role 99–100
Morphet, Prof. J., *The Role of Chief
    Executives in Local
    Government* 3, 50, 65, 70, 71,
    104
Morris, R., *A muddle over monitors*
    100

Networking 83–4
Northampton guidelines, member–
    employee relations 116–18
Norton, A.
    *The Role of Chief Executive in
        British Local Government* 65,
        104
    *The Town Clerk: The Nature of the
        Role and its Contribution to
        British Local Government* 104

Opposition groups, relationship with
   chief executive 56
Opposition leader, relationship with
   chief executive 54
Organisational commitment 110

Party group meetings 95–8, 117
Paterson Report 1
   The New Scottish Local Authorities
      15
Pay 16
Performance review 77–8
Personal image projection 30
Personal publicity profile 98–9
Personal style 28
Political impartiality 50, 117
Political leaderships 50–7
   leader of council 51–4
Political outlook 40–1
Political realities 87
Powers 16
Practices, 'the 27' 111–12
Predecessor 101–2
Press 63
Private interest conflict 5
Privatisation 94–5
Professional development 7
Proportionality rules 50
Public scrutiny 40–3

Qualifications required 2–3
Qualities required 4, 6

Reasons for becoming a chief
      executive 3–5
Relationships
   with chief officers 57–61
   with controlling groups 55–6
   with employees 61–2
   with independents 56–7
   with leader of council 51–4
   with opposition groups 56
   with opposition leader 54
   with other party leaders 54–5

political leaderships 50–7
   with press 63
   with town clerk 116–17
   with trade unions 62–3
Religious attendances 89–90
Revans, R.W. 82
Role 65–75
   budget process 66
   employee development 67–8
   handling negotiations 66–7
   managing members 68–75
   monitoring officer 99–100

Self-confidence 109
Self-management 109
SOLACE 83, 99
   *Chief Executives' Development
      Effectiveness* study 10
   counselling service 13
   description 12–13
   formation 1
   foundation 12
   guidelines on hospitality and gifts
      113–15
   meaning of chief executive 1
   objects 13
   overseas activities 13
   papers 105–7
   professional development 7
   recognition of experience 9
   *Recruiting and Selecting a Chief
      Executive: Guidelines for good
      practice* 15
   recruitment and selection service
      15–16
   *Training Needs of the Newly
      Appointed Chief Executive* 29
SOLACE International (1992) Ltd
      13
South Africa, town clerkship
      qualification 7
Special responsibility allowance,
      leader of council 52
Standing orders 100–1

Stewart, Prof. J., *The Role of the Chief Executive* 65
Strategic management 111
Stress 4–5, 43–7
  chief executive causing 45–7
  management 109
  and pressure 44

Team management 109
Time management 26, 84–5
Town clerk 116–17
Trade unions,
  accessibility of chief executive 72–3
  relationship with chief executive 62–3

USA
  International City-County Management Association (ICMA) 8–9, 112
  local government 8

Widdicombe Report 57
Woodroffe, 'Competent by any other name' 8
Working Party on Internal Management of Local Authorities, *Community Leadership and Representation* 50
Working week, number of hours 44